I Remember

A Practical Guide to Self-Realization

David Lee Sheng Tin, HHC, Ph.D

PRAISE FOR I REMEMBER

Have you ever found yourself in a whirl of negative thoughts and clueless about what to do to lift yourself out of the dungeon of disastrous and debilitating negative wallowing? David Lee Sheng Tin's I Remember: A Practical Guide to Self-Realization might be the lever you need to pull you up and anchor you in a place that is steady, serene, and spacious. I Remember provides a valuable toolbox of options for developing an introspective and positive attitude as a way of life.

This book explores the self as mind, body, intellect, feelings, emotions, and ego. Lee Sheng Tin dwells upon the philosophy that the body is an energy field that interacts with chemicals, food, light, and sound, and thus these very elements can promote healing or harm to the body depending on their usage. The author delves into the yoga philosophy of the five koshas: Ananda Mayakosha, Vijayanagar Kosha, and ManomayaKosha. Pranamayakosha and Annamayakosha.

Emotional health, according to Lee Sheng Tin, consists of self-awareness, empathy, adaptability, optimism, faith, and the possession of an analytical mind. I Remember examines the benefits of transcendental meditation on the body and promotes Ayurveda geared towards the reprogramming of one's mind towards positivity by using visualization, meditation, and positive affirmation.

Young people who are attempting to understand their identity and destiny will benefit immensely from the practical steps advised in this book. People open to understanding the common spirituality that pervades the diverse religious dogmas and practices will find this text particularly insightful. Any individual interested in developing self-esteem, self-control, and self-appreciation will appreciate the discussions that emanate from this text. The following are some words of wisdom shared in I Remember:

"We have seen that the rise to higher states of consciousness opens the awareness to a greater appreciation of God's creation of others and increases our love, understanding, and compassion. Self-realization, therefore, fulfills the goal of all religions to grow in love, peace, happiness, and goodwill toward all."

The narratives shared in this book are nothing short of enlightening and create peaceful emanations in the exercise of close reading. Paulette Reefer from Reedsy.com

"I Remember" is an interesting and comprehensive book, filled with knowledge on dealing with life. In the book David wakes people up and teaches you how to deal with life issues. He gives new meaning to life and how to live it". ...Cristie Sebastian, N.C. U.S.A.

"Love the book! Many of us are on the path of growth, but sometimes we forget important things and still get confused what are the right choices. This book is a great reminder and full of good tips, directions and exercises that help us to get back on the right track." Snježana Petrovski, Meditation Teacher, *Croatia*

"I Remember " is an excellent read for anyone looking to help themselves achieve Self- knowledge and enlightenment. It presents in easy to read terms truths about life and offers practical techniques for improving one's life on

the spiritual, emotional, mental, behavioral and physical levels. I highly recommend everyone read it"… Joe Innella, Entrepreneur, S.C U.S.A.

Dr.Lee gives us a good overview of the journey towards Self Realization or as Maslow called it Self Actualization in his famous hierarchy of needs. The huge difference is that Maslow said that only 2 % of the population can achieve it. Dr.Lee refers to his spiritual teacher who said that it is everyone's birthright. Dr. Lee then maps out a way to achieve it with scientific research to support technologies he proposes. Dr. Jim Bagnola, Author of "Becoming A Professional Human Being".

This is one of best self -help guides for inner transformation and spiritual development that I have ever come across! It satisfies my hunger for at least a deep intellectual understanding of my spirituality but more it offers practical ways and programs to take big concrete steps of evolution toward achieving the promise of integrating that understanding into my daily experiences and permanently living the higher love intuition and enhanced sensory perceptions of advanced spirituality in a synthesis of body mind and Being that is 24 hours of bliss stabilized! Frank Carpenter, Meditation Teacher, Iowa, USA

ISBN 978-1-957582-36-8 (paperback)
ISBN 978-1-957582-37-5 (digital)

SECOND EDITION

Printed in the United States of America

WESTPOINT
PRINT AND MEDIA

CONTENTS

To,

The seekers of enlightenment and self-realization

ACKNOWLEDGEMENTS

This book, I Remember, would not have been possible without the knowledge and experiences I have gained from my years of involvement in teaching and practicing Transcendental Meditation (TM), as well as the guidance and teachings of Maharishi Mahesh Yogi, the founder of TM.

To the many friends and associates who have shared this journey of self-realization with me over the years, I say, thank you for being there. A special thanks to Richard Robertson, Frank Carpenter, Joe Innella, and Margo Baum, for allowing me to share their experiences of growth in the book. You have given life to the information in the book.

To Amerone Wajadally, and others who have taken the time to review and advise on the initial drafts, thank you all for your valuable insights in making this work a reality.

Finally, to all who have touched my life and made me who I am, I am grateful for having met you on life s journey. You have taught me how to be and not be through the experiences we shared. Every experience in my life has assisted me to grow, evolve. I learned so much from the apparent negative experiences. They made me realize that I was looking in the wrong places and faces for happiness, love, and peace. Those experiences became the stepping stones to a greater realization of myself as a divine being.

To my family, my daughter Devina and all who loved me and I love, thank you for allowing me to share my love with you. May you continue to unfold your enlightened self and share the love that you are with the world.

INTRODUCTION

Self-realization has been the goal of many spiritual seekers throughout the ages. However, a very few of them are familiar with what the Self is? What can one do to realize it, and what is the importance of know thy self? Self-realization is a term that is often used in western philosophy as a way to describe the fulfillment of one's full potential. In eastern philosophy, Self-realization describes that state of life where the individual lives in harmony with the laws of nature or the laws of God in the full realization of his oneness and connection with the universe.

Discoveries of modern science in Quantum Physics and its understanding of the universe offer an insight into the Self. This understanding of the Self and the universe corresponds to the description that is given to us by spiritual masters throughout the ages. The masters spoke of a field of life beyond the field of our normal sensory perception, which is the source of everything in the universe. Some called it the Absolute, the Kingdom of Heaven, Nirvana, and Sat Chit Ananda. The description is the same, though the name may be different. The masters and saints have advised that we should seek that first if we want to be free from suffering and have a blissful life.

Who am I, and what is the nature of myself? These are a couple of questions I started asking from a very young age? I was in my early teens when I first heard about self-realization. One of my tutors introduced me to the concept during one of our discussions about life. His simple explanation was, self-realization is about knowing about yourself. He was not wrong, but his definition was not very helpful, maybe because I find it a little incomplete at that time. It became clear to me after I had experiences of silence and inner awareness during meditation.

I was fortunate to learn meditation in my early twenties. I studied and worked under a great master of consciousness, Maharishi Mahesh Yogi, the founder of Transcendental Meditation, for over twenty-five years. With regular practice of meditation, my experiences and knowledge of self-realization became clearer.

A few individuals are fortunate enough to be born with an awakened awareness and in a nourishing environment that is favorable to progress their material and spiritual growth. However, the vast majority have to work to achieve a measure of material and spiritual success in life. Education and the past successes of others offer guidelines for those seeking material success in their chosen field. However, the path of spiritual growth has not been clear for most, as there still exists a lot of confusion in understanding what spiritual growth is.

Some rely on their religion and faith to provide the answer, while others turn to meditation and new age thinking on spirituality and enlightenment. They seek to connect with a divine or universal source. There are various ways to achieve enlightenment. However, just like in our material quest, there are more efficient methods and knowledge that can help you achieve the goal faster.

In pursuing material success, we need proper knowledge and direct experience to succeed. The same can be said for spiritual growth. With no direct experience and only intellectual understanding, we will become armchair philosophers.

The goal of this book is to offer individuals who are interested in spiritual development an insight into some practical steps that are necessary to awaken the memory of your true nature.

To become self-realized, it is important to remember your true nature as a divine being. Throughout the book, I share personal experiences I have had of growing to higher states of awareness or consciousness and the positive effects it has brought about in my life. These experiences and changes are not unique to me but are happening to many people from all walks of life. They helped me remember my true nature.

We all want to be happy, to experience growth and love in life. This is the desire of everyone. We are born to be happy, to be free, and to grow in love and fulfillment unfortunately, many people struggle to fulfill these basic needs.

In this book, you will learn how to overcome the feelings of lack of growth and freedom by discovering your true self. On your journey, you discover that we are not just physical beings with a physical body; we are also spiritual or light beings that have created a physical form, the body, and mind, to move and interact on this physical planet we call earth.

You may notice that "self" is sometimes used with an uppercase "S" and at other times with a lowercase "s" in the book. The word Self is used to describe the universal Field, the Absolute. When its spell with a small s, the self describes the individual ego, for example, myself, which differs from the universal ego or Self.

Understanding the self means understanding all aspects of the self - mind, body, intellect, feeling, emotions, and ego. I invite you to come with me as we explore each area and discover techniques that we can use to develop and unfold these areas. These are known as sheaths (koshas) in yoga physiology.

Following is a brief description of the five sheaths.
[1]The 5 sheaths (Koshas)

1. Annamaya Kosha: The outer sheath is the body layer muscles, bones, skin, organs. Anna means food, which is what sustains this level.
2. Pranamaya Kosha: The next sheath is the life force/energy sheath. It has to do with the breath and the flow of energy through the body.
3. Manomaya Kosha: The next sheath is the mind or mental sheath. It has to do with thoughts and emotions.
4. Vijnanamaya Kosha: This is the knowledge sheath. This kosha comprises your wisdom, intuition, and perception.
5. Anadamaya Kosha: The innermost sheath is the bliss sheath. It represents unending joy, love, peace, and complete happiness. This book covers each of the above areas, offering understanding and techniques to help unfold your full potential.

---

[1] The Koshas of the Human Body in Yoga
By Ann Pizer Reviewed by Kristin McGee, CPT on June 03, 2020

CHAPTER 1

Who Am I?

As a boy, I remember gazing at the stars and asking, why are we born? And what is the purpose of life?

Like most people, the answer to the question Who am I? was through association with family, society, and culture. I identified as a Trinidadian male of Chinese and Scottish descent. I grew up in a lower-middle-class family where money was always short. My father worked hard in his restaurant to make ends meet. My life situation and society suggested that if you do well in school, secure a good-paying job, have a successful career, and follow your religion, you will have freedom and happiness.

Around the age of fourteen, my beliefs started to shift. My curiosity to find the true purpose of life led me to explore the philosophies and writings, and teachings of various religions. From my study of martial arts, I discovered that there was an energy force called Chi that you can cultivate to increase your power and strength. The masters used meditation and breathing techniques to enliven this force within.

Many of the philosophies from East and West also spoke about knowing the Self. "Know Thy Self" is a common phrase that is written above the entrance to the temple of Delphi in Greece many centuries ago. The Vedic masters and spiritual leaders from the East spoke of Nirvana,

Sat Chit Ananda, and self-realization as places within one's conscious mind you can experience through meditation.

The Christians spoke of a Kingdom of Heaven within oneself as a place where All will be granted to you. But, what was the nature of the Self that the philosophers spoke of? Could this be the answer to the question Who am I?

With awakened curiosity, I read more on the subject and soon discovered that the Self is formless, beyond the conscious level of the mind. What Western philosophers called the ego, Eastern philosophy refers to it as the individual self or atman. When we say I, the I referred to is the self. In Eastern philosophy, the self is beyond the physical body and thoughts but is the thinker, the I, that generates the thought, who am I?. The self or I is an expression of an infinite source of universal energy and intelligence from which everything in the universe emerged, just like a river flowing out of the ocean. This concept was fascinating to me.

It was not until I started meditation in my early twenties that the experience and knowledge of the Self became clearer to me. I read The Physics of Tao by Fritjof Capra (Fritjof, 1975) and The Dancing Wu Li Masters by Gary Zukav (Zukav, 1979). These books offered explanations of the structure of the universe and the building blocks of all life in the universe. This later became my introduction to Physics and Quantum Field Theory. Given below is a summary of modern science and its understanding of the universe and the physical body that helped me in my quest of finding the answer to Who am I?

Modern understanding of the universe

In 1905, Albert Einstein published his Special Theory of Relativity and changed the way scientists viewed the world. Before this time, most scientists held a Newtonian view of the world where everything is seen objectively, and they considered all physical reactions to being due to physical causes. An example is balls colliding on a pool table, causing a physical reaction between the balls. The world was solid, with solid physical systems interacting with each other, creating cause-and-effects that could be seen and measured. This view helped explain the motions of the planets, mechanical machines, and fluids in continuous motion. However, in the early nineteenth century, Michael Faraday and James Maxwell's discovery of electromagnetism and force fields changed the view of a purely mechanical world to one where the universe is composed of energy fields that create forces interacting with each other.

Science describes a field as a condition in space that has the potential of producing a force. The concept of a universe filled with energy fields that create forces interacting with each other gave the scientific framework to explain how we can affect each other at a distance through means other than sight and speech.

In the early 1900s, an alternative theory called Quantum Physics emerged. This further changed our concept of reality and ourselves. Quantum physics states that mass and energy are interchangeable, and consequently, that mass is merely a manifestation of energy. This implies that everything, including our body, is simply energy stored in mass particle form.

Another discovery of Quantum physics is that the observer or experimenter observing the object affects the object. The light from his/her eyes (sight) falling on an object affects the energy field of the object.

Physicists, such as Dr. David Bohm, state that there are no basic building blocks of matter; instead, the universe is inseparable as a whole. It is a vast web of interacting interweaving probabilities (Dr. Bohm, 1981).

Energy Fields

According to the theories associated with the universal energy field, all matter and psychological processes thoughts, emotions, beliefs, and attitudes are made of energy. When applied to the human body, every atom, molecule, cell, tissue, and body system is energy that, when superimposed on each other, creates the human energy field.

The view that the universe is comprised of energy fields is not new. In the third millennium B.C., the Chinese said that all matter is energy and is pervaded by universal energy called Chi or life force.

Around 538 B.C., the Jewish mystical theosophy, Kabbalah, refers to these energies as the astral light. Almost all religions and spiritual organizations, Christian, Vedic, Jewish, Chinese, Native American, Buddhists, the Rosicrucian, state that there is a universal energy field pervading everything in the universe. In his book, Future Science, John White (White, 1977) lists ninety-seven different cultures that refer to aura phenomena by ninety-seven different names. Modern science now recognizes the same truth; the human energy field is the manifestation of universal energy intimately involved with human life.

We now know that everything in the universe, including the human body, comprises energy fields. The energy causes the tides to flow, the clouds to move, the plant and our body to grow and to transform. The amount of energy a system has, the more powerful it will be. For instance, the amount of energy in a tornado or hurricane, the more powerful it will be.

A body at rest has potential energy. As it releases the energy from its resting state, it transforms the body. The faster the release of energy, the more powerful the transformation will be. The energy in the universe moves in spirals. When we examine the growth of a tree, we see the rings are all in circles, smaller on the inner, and it gets larger as the circles expand outwards. The same is true of the milky way, a hurricane, a tornado, and the energy in our body and in all things. To grow and evolve, we need more than just energy; we also need intelligence to give that energy a direction. Without intelligence, energy could flow in a chaotic manner.

How can we increase energy in ourselves? We know from experience that we gain energy from rest. The deeper we rest, the more energy we gain. Furthermore, to use the energy we gain from rest, we have to move. Movement causes energy to flow. When we wake in the morning, we naturally stretch because stretching causes the energy to move.

Physics tells us that energy cannot be destroyed but can be transformed. The foundation of all creation is the same; it is a constant field of potential energy from which all forms and matter in the universe are emerging and collapsing at an infinite speed. Energy expresses itself from the unified field as light. As light spirals out, it fractures into the various colors of the rainbow. Each color has a particular sound or vibration. The further that energy moves from its source, the slower the vibration or speed gets. This slowing down of the vibration produces form or matter.

Consciousness

Consciousness simply means awareness. We usually are aware of things, for instance, a rose, the room, a person. For this to happen, there are three things involved:

- The person who is aware of their surroundings; we can call that person the experiencer.
- The object of observation, for example, the rose.
- The means or process through which the person perceives the object.

When we close our eyes in meditation, the object of perception becomes our thoughts. We know from experience that thoughts come from deep within the mind, experienced first as a faint idea or feeling and then expressed as words. Thoughts have energy and intelligence. The energy causes the thought to move from more profound levels of the mind to the conscious level, and intelligence gives it direction. Therefore, the source of thought must be infinite field or source of intelligence and energy within us. Since thoughts have been coming into the mind since we were born, there must be an infinite, never-ending source of thoughts deep within the mind.

As we turn our attention inward during meditation and allow the mind to follow the path of the development of thought, the mind experiences more silent and deeper areas of itself as it experiences subtler levels of the thinking process. The mind then reaches the most refined or subtlest level of the thinking process and goes beyond the finest level or experience of the thought.

At this stage, the object of observation the thought has disappeared, and therefore the individual s mind is without any object to experience. In this state, the awareness or consciousness is pure, meaning that one is aware of nothing in particular but is just fully awake or aware within himself; that fully awake state of consciousness is the state of self-realization.

The experience refreshes the mind and body, creating greater awareness and clarity of thinking, bringing more energy and creativity to daily life.[2] Having dipped deep into the source of thoughts, the mind and body get infused with the energy, with the intelligence available at the source of thoughts. You cannot enter the ocean and not get wet.

---

[2] Scientific Research on Maharishi s Transcendental Meditation Program: Collected Papers, Volume 1 (Rheinweiler, Germany: Maharishi Research University): 396-399,1977 International Journal Of Neuroscience 13: 211-217, 1981.

Experiencing the Self

As my mind settled down during my meditation, I became aware that my body was vibrating energy, and the energy throughout my body was flowing through the top of my head and connecting with an infinite source of the energy field of pure light that was around me; above, below, and inside me, all at the same time, covering me from all 360 angles. I felt connected to this source of light and energy, like a river that flows into the sea and out of the sea at the same time.

My body was more light energy than physical, and I could direct the energy up and down my physical self as I pleased. I felt at perfect peace and silence that was unbounded and blissful. The thinking was a faint idea or intention rather than an expressed thought. I felt at one with everything. After meditation, the feeling of oneness continues. Even though I still perceive objects in my surroundings as being solid yet, on a faint level, I am acutely aware of the space in which everything exists, including myself, and that space is the same that is within me. There is a sense of unity pervading my perception and a connection with all that I perceive. I am more aware of the light around objects and individuals, and I recognize that it is the same light that I am.

This experience gave me the answer to my question who am I?

I now know both from science and my own personal experience I am a being of light energy that is an expression of a universal field of light energy pervading everything in the universe. What I am is true for everyone; only we have to know how to enliven it in our awareness. This level of myself I call my Divinity. Others call it the self, soul, or atman.

The Nature of the Self

What is the self? Is it the body, our thoughts, feelings, emotions, memories, and desires? Even though all these are parts of our self, it can t be the total answer. Our body is constantly changing itself every seven years. Our thoughts and emotions change every day. Nothing in the relative field of life is ever constant or non-changing, yet we feel that there is a deeper part of us that never changes, despite the fact that our physical bodies may change. It is the essential nature of our being. But the question is, What is Being?

Maharishi Mahesh Yogi, the founder of TM, describes Being in his book, The Science of Being and Art Of Living (Yogi, Science of Being and Art of Living, 1963-2001), as, Underneath the subtlest layer of all that exists in the relative field is the abstract, absolute field of Being, which is unmanifested and transcendental. It is neither matter nor energy. It is pure Being, the state of pure existence. This state of pure existence underlies all that exists. Everything is the expression of this pure existence or absolute Being which is the essential constituent of all relative life.

Maharishi s description of Being is like the scientist s description of the Unified Field as described before.

To be is to exist. The state of Being, according to Maharishi, is the state of pure existence. We are like waves of expressions on the surface of the ocean of Being. Each expression has its unique form, but all come from the same source. At the point of emergence from the state of pure existence, Being-becomes-takes a specific form, like the wave rising from the ocean. This becoming is the first expression of the individual self. The recognition of I am.

As the mind settles down to its least excited state during meditation, the individual experiences himself as one with Being the field of existence. He realizes himself to be nothing other than an expression of a universal field of intelligence. This inner experience is one of unboundedness, silence, peace, and bliss. This is the state of self-realization. To know this, one has to become it. It in itself is proof of itself.

Self-realization is another state of awareness that differs from waking, dreaming, and sleep states we are all accustomed to. Just as waking, dreaming, and sleeping states have different physiological correlates, similarly, the state of self-realization has different physiological correlations. (Wallace,1971). During meditation, the regular experience of this state restructures the physiology by purifying the mind and body and increasing brain coherence. This allows the individual to live a heightened state of awareness in daily life.

CHAPTER 2

Ananda Mayakosha– The Bliss Sheath

The Awakening

My introduction to meditation was not intended, but just by chance. A friend who was a little older called me one day all excited and said, David, I found what we are looking for. Come and see me later today. Curious to know what he was speaking about, I visited him at his home later that day. It was then he told me about meditation and how it had helped him overcome his anxiety and gave him more energy. We were both involved in sports and martial arts and were always looking for ways to improve our performance. On his advice, I started Transcendental Meditation, TM, to boost my performance.

Soon after starting mediation, I became ill with a contagious disease. It all started with my visit to a friend's home. His mother greeted me with a kiss and exclaimed, David, you have a fever!

I was surprised and denied that it was true as I was feeling good. However, she checked my temperature and she was right. I surely had a high fever! The following day, I visited the doctor and discovered I had tuberculosis. In the 1970s, TB was considered a very contagious and sometimes fatal disease. I was shocked and confused and wondered, why me?

I was having fun, doing regular exercise, had a good job, and spent my weekends at the beach and at parties with friends. Life was good. I learned that I had to be institutionalized and all my friends and co-workers had to be tested. This made me depressed and anxious about my future. It felt like my life had ended.

I spent over three months isolated in a hospital. During my time of isolation, I meditated every day and found an undiscovered level of peace and silence within myself that was very nourishing and enjoyable. This place of silence existed within when my mind became free of thoughts and entered a state of pure awareness.

As a young man who just had his life turned upside down because of illness, this became my go-to place for solace, peace, and comfort. I also noticed that even though I was ill and had very few visitors, I felt happy and contented, despite my isolation. This was contrary to what I expected. My room in the hospital was between the asthmatic and heart wards, where a patient would die every day. As a young person, having to deal with death daily made me realize how unpredictable life was. I would see and talk to a patient one day, and the next day I would learn that he passed away. This experience made me once more question the purpose of life.

On leaving the hospital a few months later, I returned to my normal life with a new outlook. My regular meditations opened my awareness to an inner reality of peace and happiness that I was unaware of before. The world seemed brighter. Looking at the mountains, I was more aware of the space that existed between the hills and the distance between the clouds and the sky. Of course, it was always that way, but I guess I was too busy with my own thoughts and rushing about to notice them before. At work, I realized how unhappy most people were and how they would get upset about minor challenges in life. I realized that before meditation, I also behaved in that way. This was the start of my awakening.

Over the years, as I became a teacher of TM and instructed others, I realized my initial experience of inner peace and happiness was and is a common phenomenon with most new meditators. Jack Forem (Forem, 2012), in his book Transcendental Meditation, shares many similar experiences of meditators during their initial days of meditating.

I became more involved in teaching and lecturing, gaining more knowledge and experience of this inner state of life that I learned was the field of pure consciousness or pure awareness that the spiritual masters spoke of.

I was fortunate to have worked and studied under a great spiritual teacher and foremost leader in consciousness, Maharishi Mahesh Yogi, the founder of Transcendental Meditation. Maharishi spoke about the field of pure consciousness and offered techniques and courses to help enhance the experience. He also invited leading scientists and researchers in health, Quantum Field theory, and neurophysiology to research TM and explain the link between consciousness and the Unified Field of Quantum Mechanics. Having attended many of these lectures and courses over the years, the experience of my inner self became much clearer. I filled my life with creative activities and joy.

However, my bubble of bliss busted. After eighteen years of marriage, my partner walked out of the relationship, taking our only child with her. This was unexpected, as for all intents and purpose, I felt we had a good marriage. This sudden loss once more threw my life in a spin. All my hopes for the future swiftly disappeared. I was not sure of what my future hold from this point forward. I remember sitting alone in our home with the rain falling and feeling the emptiness and silence of the house. In that silence, I closed my eyes to search for peace and meditated. As my mind transcended, an inner feeling of peace and silence replaced the emptiness I felt. In that stillness, I felt embraced by light, expansion, and fullness that I could only describe as love.

Coming out of meditation, the reality of what occurred and my life situation came flooding back. The only thing different this time was that I felt nourished by divine love and presence that was not there before. This awareness was strange to me. It seemed like I was existing in a strange state. I was very conscious of all the things that were taking place and had to deal with it, and yet, I felt removed from it all. If I closed my eyes, there was peace and love; when I opened my eyes, there was chaos, loss of love, and everything I worked for. This new awareness allowed me to handle my divorce in a more amicable way that would otherwise not be possible. At the end of the divorce, I lost everything; home, money, child, and friends.

Left without a home, money, and with few friends to turn to, I became more aware of my inner self and learned more about the creative potential that I have. From being penniless and under heavy debt, I rebuilt my life and finances in a few short years. This enabled me to take my young daughter every year on a month-long trip, visiting various cities and countries around the world.

This second awakening showed me that my inner life was divine. It reminded me that everything outside myself was subject to change at any moment. Without knowing the deeper levels of my consciousness, I would suffer the fate of pain and anxiety of the many who experience loss and disappointment in life. I still had to deal with the challenges of divorce, finance, relationships, etc., but the inner peace, love, and joy, which was becoming my constant companion, allowed me to overcome these obstacles and grow without the trauma and pain.

In the years following my divorce, my inner and outer life experiences continued to expand. I gained new skills and knowledge and furthered my studies in natural medicine while building my coaching and consulting business. I formed new relationships and traveled the world, teaching and enjoying making new friends in many countries. My level of inner contentment, peace, and happiness continued to grow along with a deeper understanding and experience of who I am at my core. I knew and appreciated through direct experience that the silence, joy, and freedom within was the source of my physical self, and I felt its presence more and more throughout the activity.

A feeling of inner silence and awareness accompanied my daily activities regardless of how active or inactive I was. I was enjoying every bit of it. Once the moment passed, I did not feel any attachment or long for it, even if it was gratifying. I filled my days with creative ideas. I designed and taught courses, hiked, visited foreign places, and had fun with friends. My life was glorious!

By 2012, I was in a wonderful place. I felt a deep connection with the universe and was at peace with all that had happened in my life so far. I felt I had fulfilled my life s purpose and was content to leave life if it were to happen.

I traveled to India with some friends to attend the Kumbh Mela the following year; the Kumbh Mela is a Vedic festival that is held every twelve years in Allahabad. One night, while staying at a hotel in the countryside outside of the major city, I slipped, fell ten feet, and landed at the bottom of a flight of marble steps. This happened while walking and talking on the garden grounds of the hotel where we were staying.

It was a moonless night. The garden in which we were walking was lit by a few dim lights that were scattered around the area. Suddenly, the lights went out, and we stepped into the darkness, unaware of our path; we had approached the ledge where the stairs began; there was no barrier of any kind to prevent you from falling over the ledge onto the flight of stairs. Unaware of the ledge, I stepped forward and descended into the darkness.

When my body contacted the hard marble steps, I felt every cell in my body react! My consciousness slipped out-of-body awareness into the transcendental field that I was now so familiar with. I experienced pure light and complete freedom, and unboundedness. This lasted only for a moment, but for me, it seemed like a long time.

As my awareness returned to my body, I became aware that I could not move my legs. People rushed down the stairs to assist, but I told them to give me a moment as I tried to figure out where I was hurt. They lifted me up and took me into the lobby of the hotel, where they placed me on a couch. As I lay down, I felt I was going into shock. My entire body was feeling cold, and I shook. My friend became alarmed, and I could see how worried he looked. I was aware of what was happening to my physical self, but I saw the room and my body as vibrating particles of energy. My attention shifted to my legs, and I could see how the energy field that was my leg was excited. I placed my hands and attention on my leg and directed the energy to settle down. This had a calming effect on my whole physiology and allowed my awareness to return to normal.

Regardless of the pain and immobility I experienced during the initial weeks of my accident, I never felt unhappy or disturbed. I continued to wonder why I was still alive as I felt certain that I could have died. It was a time of introspection, a time to review my life and chart a new course and purpose.

It took me a few months to recover fully from my fall. The experience shifted my awareness once again. Since that time, I have felt I had a rebirth. Consciousness continues to expand rapidly, and a growing sense of oneness and connection with everything pervades activity. I feel closer to the universe and identify more with the inner reality of myself and the universe than with the outer reality of activity and form. There is an inner feeling of love for all and inner fullness that is constant. Even though I still have responsibilities in relative life, somehow, the worries associated with the challenges of life are no longer present. I feel and believe that The Lord is my Shepard and I shall not want. This ongoing awareness is my constant reminder that I am more than just a physical body; that my inner divine nature is the source and goal of all that I am or hoped to be in life. This was another level of awakening that keeps on growing, which changed the perception and understanding of reality that I had.

I Remember

Over the course of the years, I realized that every loss or tragedy pushed me closer to the memory of my true self. It was nature's way of telling me that the happiness and love I was seeking in the outer sphere of life were not permanent and could change at a moment's notice; that only with an awareness of the self and awakening to the full value of happiness and love that exist within, you can experience complete fulfillment. These experiences enlivened the memory of my true nature. That is why all the great teachers said, To seek that first. I now know that bliss consciousness can be a living reality for everyone, and we are all born to live and enjoy the fullness of our inner life.

The experiences of growing consciousness are not unique to me, even though circumstances may be different. In fact, many people from all around the world are waking up to the awareness of the beauty of their inner self. The following experiences are from participants who attended a course on TM and its advanced program, the TM Sidhis program at the Maharishi International University, Fairfield, Iowa, USA. (Management, 2012)

"During my TM program, my awareness was lively and settled. The state was timeless- I felt a beautiful shower of soft, silver streams coming from above. It was so delightful when the rain-like streams entered my body in cooling, healing streams. They went to a part of the body that had some imbalance. A long-term pain was instantaneously and naturally removed by these streams. As the waves washed through me, I realized that they were streaming from within my Self and permeating my whole Being, from subtle to gross levels of my individuality.

For the next week, I felt as though the ocean had come to my door. Every time I closed my eyes, I fell into a smooth, warm, rapturous state. The only word for it was ecstasy". N.C.

The experiences of Bliss, peace, freedom, and love are the reality of the Self; the field of Anandamaya kosha.

The science behind Transcendental Meditation

Over the past fifty years, many scientific research studies have been conducted on the effectiveness of the TM program and how they are associated with enhancing and enriching all levels of life; mind, body, behavior, and environment. These researches are published in peer research journals and are documented in a set of seven volumes of scientific research papers.

The research revealed that during the TM technique, the mind and body experience this deep state of rest. The deep rest and energy purify the physiology, dissolves stress, and increases the coherence in the brain, allowing the energy output in the brain to become more balanced and equalized. As a result, the individual experiences increased intelligence, creativity, and reduction of stress and anxiety.[3]

---

[3] Scientific Research on Maharishi s Transcendental Meditation Program: Collected Papers, Volume 1 (Rheinweiler, Germany: Maharishi Research University): 396-399,1977
International Journal Of Neuroscience 13: 211-217, 1981.
American Psychologist 42: 879-881, 1987

Meditation

The Transcendental Meditation (TM) technique is a simple, natural, effortless, mental technique anyone can practice, including children from the age of five. It requires no change in religious beliefs, diet, or lifestyle and is practiced for twenty minutes twice a day while sitting comfortably with eyes closed. TM spontaneously leads the mind to fathom the deeper levels of thought toward its source. This activates or awakens the deeper levels of consciousness. The experience gives the individual the ability to use more of these subtle levels of the mind in activity and, with regular practice, leads to higher states of consciousness.

TM is the first step on the path to self-realization. The advanced TM techniques help to enhance the meditation experiences by clearing the horizontal levels of the mind, allowing the mind to experience subtle levels of creation as it transcends. The more advanced TM-Sidhi program trains the mind to think and act from the level of pure consciousness, the field of all possibilities.

We could compare meditation to watering the root of a plant. If the soil is fertile and the seed is perfect, all you have to do is water the root twice daily, and you will have a perfect tree. Watering the root is the primary activity that a farmer has to do to sustain the plant's life. Regular meditation is also the primary activity we must undertake to live a peaceful, fulfilling life. However, like most trees, we need more than just water twice a day to grow strong and perfect. We also need to know how to take care of other parts of our mind and body. As with a plant, we need to understand the nature of the soil, climate, and surroundings for the plant to grow correctly, we also need to understand what the body, mind, and emotions are missing and what we can do to quickly achieve the goal of self-realization.

As effective as meditation is in improving physical and mental health, some meditators continue to experience moments of depression and have difficulty in maintaining relationships, worry about the future, and wonder if they will ever achieve enlightenment. For instance, Jane keeps wondering what is wrong with her. Why after all these years, she is still not enlightened and continues to struggle with occasional depression and anxiety. She believes that her meditation has been helpful, but she feels that she is not achieving the higher levels of consciousness and inner fulfillment that she has heard about. I have heard this story from a number of people over the years. These people are true seekers of enlightenment who, after many years on a spiritual path, start to doubt if they will ever achieve their goal.

Sometimes, people in spiritual and religious communities who are experiencing a lack of growth tend to indulge in spiritual bypass. A term developed by John Welwood, the author of Journey of the heart: The path of conscious Love.

Welwood describes spiritual bypass as using spiritual ideas and practices to sidestep personal, emotional unfinished business, to shore up a shaky sense of self, or belittle basic needs, feelings and developmental tasks, all in the name of enlightenment.

They fake it to make it. To fit in with their community of spiritual seekers, they pretend that everything is alright and their life is blissful.

Layers of consciousness

You don't have to become enlightened; you have to remove the blocks that hinder you from experiencing and living your already enlightened state.

Our body and mind are made up of many layers or sheaths. Just as the various colors of light are expressions of pure white light vibrating at a slower speed, the various sheaths of mind and body are expressions of the unified field or pure consciousness vibrating at a slower speed. It is like the sap in a plant that expresses itself as leaves, stem, flower, etc. Each sheath is a layer of vibrating energy and each layer has to be fully enlivened to permanently live the state of enlightenment.

Enlightenment or self-realization is the natural state of our life. However, to unfold it, each layer of our physiology needs to be purified and nourished. You don't have to become enlightened; you have to remove the blocks that hinder you from experiencing and living your already enlightened state. As many have experienced, meditation alone will not achieve the goal. We also have to know how to take care of the various layers or sheaths of mind, body, and emotions.

In the next few chapters, we will examine how we can nourish the other sheaths of the body to achieve this goal.

CHAPTER 3

Vijnanamaya Kosha: The knowledge sheath

The mind has many levels. The finest level is the level of pure awareness the knowledge sheath. This level of the mind is experienced when during meditation, the mind transcends the finest level of thinking and goes beyond thought. At this level of awareness, the mind is free from all thoughts. You are just aware of the unbounded nature of the self and your connection to Being or pure consciousness. It is a state of pure awareness where there is no thought or mental activity, but you are fully awake within yourself. This is the junction point where the individual consciousness merges with and emerges from the field of pure consciousness. It is similar to the junction point where the river meets the ocean. At that point, the river has become both river and ocean at the same time. As the mind emerges from this state, the memory and intuition start to be awakened. You start to remember who you are and that you are sitting in a room meditating. From memory arises the feeling level; you now are aware that you are feeling peaceful, relaxed, etc. The next level is the thinking and discriminating level. This is the more conscious level of the mind where we may decide to continue meditating or stop and get into the activity. The memory and feeling levels are the finer aspects of the intellect.

Various Stages of Development of the Intellect

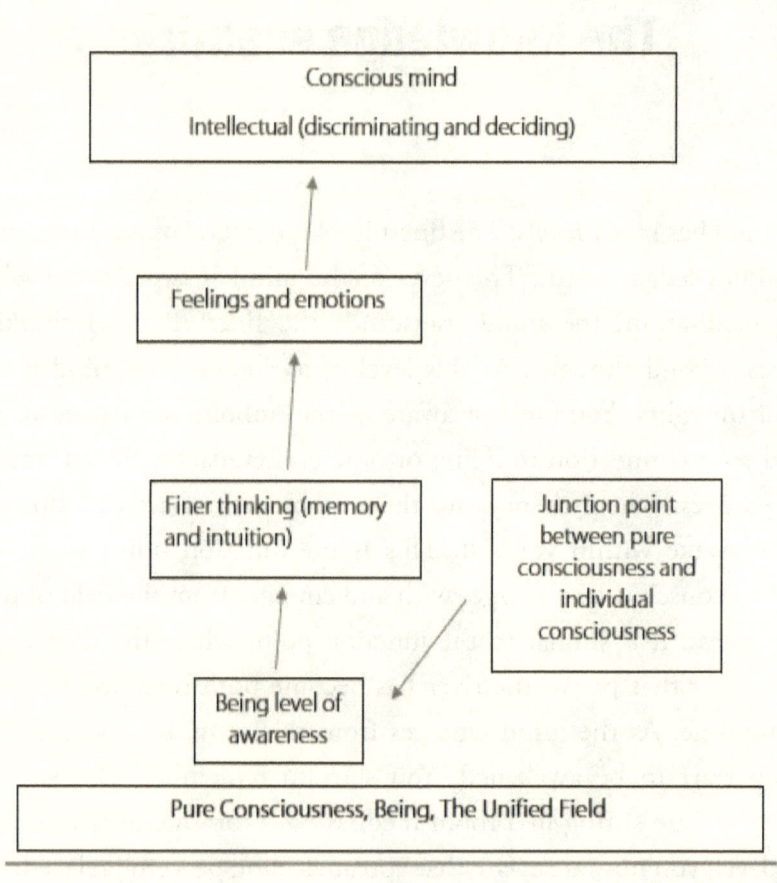

During meditation, as my mind emerges from the field of pure consciousness, I realized myself as a distinct being, I am. On this level of awareness, I am aware of I as an individual. The experience is more awareness or knowingness rather than an intellectual understanding. I feel wide awake within myself with my awareness non-localized, not focused on anything in particular. The body does not feel physical but more like vibrating energy. I realize my individual self is different from the universal Self that was just being experienced. Silence, bliss, and unboundedness of my Self, both universal and individual, are being experienced simultaneously. I compare the experience to a wave now emerging from the body of the ocean. The wave is still like a ripple on the ocean and has not yet risen in height. In this analogy, the wave on the surface of the ocean has just taken shape. In this state, I know I can know anything.

The Vedas called this level of experience Ritam Bhara Pragya. Maharishi was speaking at a lecture on the Science of Creative Intelligence (SCI) at Amherst, Massachusetts, USA, in 1971, where he said, Ritam Bhara Pragya, is that intelligence which knows only the truth (Yogi, Symposium on The Science of Creative Intelligence, 1971). According to Maharishi, when the awareness is established on this level, one feels I know everything.

In that state, I am fully conscious of the field of pure consciousness or Being and my individuality at the same time. One does not overshadow the other.

According to Maharishi, at that refined level of the mind, all knowledge is available. One only has to think, and the answer is available. This is the first sprouting of the intellect. The state of Being, pure existence, has just become, and the intelligence inherent in Being becomes the intellect of the individual.

In SCI lesson 8, Maharishi states it in this way, *"When existence becomes conscious, then intelligence becomes intelligent. This intelligent aspect of intelligence presents intelligence as creative intelligence".* This first awakening of the mind to its individual existence is the knowledge sheath, the finest level of the intellect. From here, the intellect becomes lively, and knowledge of oneself becomes lively as memory. From this memory, the level of feeling and emotions are born.

This is the awareness of the knowledge sheath, where the individual has just become conscious of himself and remembers his individuality. The analytical and feeling levels of the mind are not yet active. This is the birth of the ego or self. This is the finest level of perception at the junction point between pure consciousness and individual consciousness.

We can only know this level of life through direct experience in meditation because it is beyond the normal thinking, analytical level of the mind. Through regular meditation and experience of transcending, the mind gains the ability to stay on these fine levels and experience them clearly.

Here are a few experiences from people on an extended meditation course.

During meditation, I merged with a thick, colorless cushion of silence. My awareness watched as a small, oblong bubble of energy appeared in the vast ocean of silence. My awareness I knew that this bubble was me, that this energy was the basis of my relative form. I was just a quiet, silent observer; I knew I had always been totally one with the silence. I knew this not from memory but on the level of knowledge itself. W.H.

Whenever I sit to meditate, almost as soon as I close my eyes, a warm wave of bliss spreads out from my chest, into my arms, and eventually, my legs and head. As my meditation progresses, the world and my thoughts dissolve, and at times, it is as if the floor drops out and I fall into an expanded region of myself which has no boundaries, and which is so ecstatic that I could stay there forever, never missing anything of the outside world, including my mind!

I know that I can know anything I wish in this space, just by asking the question. I find myself smiling and laughing to myself all the time, which continues to initiate unending waves of happy, ecstatic, joyful, and bliss! Frank C. Iowa, USA.

The knowledge sheath is the first sprouting of the individual, the ego, from the unified field of pure consciousness. The advanced programs of TM allow the mind to experience these more profound levels of consciousness. For the mind to experience this level clearly, and live it in daily activity, it is necessary to purify the other levels of the physiology the feelings and emotions, intellect, energy and breath, and body. We will deal with each of these levels separately in the following chapters.

Maharishi, First International Symposium on the Science of Creative Intelligence on July 26th, 1971, at Amherst, in Massachusetts, United States.

CHAPTER 4

Manomaya Kosha: Thoughts, Feelings and Emotions

The distinction between the knowledge sheath and the feeling and emotion sheath is very fine. The awareness of "I am" almost enlivens the awareness of the feeling and emotions. The feeling is a faint idea, and emotions answer the question, "what am I feeling?" The question "what I am feeling?" raises the question "Why am I feeling this way?" This question opens the mind to intellectual analysis of the feeling and emotion and is a more gross level of the intellect or thought. We get trapped on this level, trying to understand or make sense of our feelings.

We have seen that the finest level of our thinking process is the feeling and emotional level. In actuality, it is the second most refined level of the mind and the most overlooked aspect of our self when we consider spiritual development. We take our emotions and feelings as normal, assuming that we can do little to change the way we feel. However, we all know how negative feelings and emotions can ruin our life. Therefore, we must seek ways to nourish our emotions so that the nature of ourself, bliss, can become an everyday reality of our life.

We experience thought on the feeling level as a faint idea. First, we feel, and the feeling expresses itself as an emotion. We cannot have a feeling without an emotion attached to it. Our experiences determine how we feel about events and situations in our life. We store these experiences as memory. Every memory has a feeling and emotion "happy, sad, or indifferent" attached to it.

Memory

To understand why we have certain feelings and emotions, let us look at how we create a memory. At birth, the brain has billions of neurons, but they are not all connected. Every experience changes the brain. As we grow, the neurons in the brain get connected based on our experiences. Every experience will elicit a particular feeling or set of feelings and emotions. These become the memories on which we rely when facing similar experiences. For instance, a child seeing the mother in the kitchen take flour, sugar, eggs, etc., and put them on the table, may ask, Mommy, what are you doing? The mother most likely will say, I am baking a cake. Would you like a piece later? Later, when the mother offers the child a piece of the cake, the child may find it delicious. The next time the child sees her mother place the same items on the kitchen table, she most likely will think that the mother is baking a cake. The memory of how delicious the cake was will come to the mind, and the child will wait anxiously.

A newborn mind is like a sponge, absorbing every experience. This is how we learn to identify objects, people, and harmful or delightful situations. All these experiences create a neural network that serves as the memory of who we are; our beliefs, likes, and dislikes. They create emotions that bring us joy, sorrow or pain and affect our worldview.

What pushes our emotional buttons?

Your family, culture, religion, or lack of, your education, socio-economic situation, race, and society shape your beliefs of the world and yourself and the values you hold dear. Beliefs and values affect your behavior, relationships, career, and spiritual outlook.

The meaning we attribute to certain situations in life is based on our beliefs and values, and it triggers certain emotions and feelings. For example, if you grew up in a society where the belief is that you will be unhappy if you don t have money, you may feel very stressed if you are not earning as much as your friends. Or if money was a source of conflict in your home when growing up, and your father walked out. You could assume that to have a successful marriage, you must have money. Your subconscious mind stores your beliefs and affects every level of your life. Situations and circumstances that do not fit into your belief will irritate you. Those that comply with your beliefs will please you.

The feeling level is the most tender level of life. When you feel hurt, it affects every level of your life. The same is true when our feelings are nourished. Therefore, to grow and evolve, you must learn how to nourish the feeling level in yourself and others. To achieve your goal of evolution and nourish the feeling level, the first thing to do is release the stresses that create negative thoughts and feelings. By giving deep rest to the mind and body, Transcendental Meditation (TM) dissolves stress and opens the mind to experience the deeper levels of the subconscious, transcending the feeling level and arriving at the source of thought. This inward march of the mind creates global brain coherence, balancing the energy output between the left and right hemispheres of the brain, enlivening the pre-frontal cortex, and calming the amygdala, the emotional center of the brain. This is important because the pre-frontal cortex of the brain is responsible for our sense of self, emotional intelligence, empathy, and moral reasoning. When the pre-frontal cortex goes offline due to stress, the amygdala, the fight-or-flight area of the brain, becomes hyperactive, and we become over-reactive to situations. Meditation, especially TM, has been proven to reduce stress and bring the prefrontal cortex back online.[4]

Beliefs

The beliefs you hold of yourself, your culture, and your religion structure your world. To grow and evolve, it is important to look at your beliefs and values and evaluate them to see what beliefs and values are no longer serving you and see how you can change them.

Changing your beliefs

Old beliefs are beliefs we have been expressing about ourselves and our lives. Old beliefs were passed on to us through family, society, and community. They can also come from experiences as well. Looking at the conversations you have about yourself and the world will help you identify some of your common beliefs.

We adopt beliefs early in our life, usually those which are passed on to us by our parents and other adult authority figures. As we age and mature, we may need to evaluate some of those beliefs to determine if they are working for us as adults. Here is an exercise from my book, Master Your Emotions, Transform Your Life,[5] which can help you achieve this.

---

[4] International Journal of Psychophysiology 71: 170-176, 2009 Scientific Research on Maharishi s Transcendental Meditation Program: Collected Papers, Volume 4: 2245-2266, 1989

[5] Master Your Emotions, Transform Your Life, David Lee Sheng Tin, HHC, PhD, Lulu Publishing Services, USA, 2017

Complete the following:

- List some of the family mottos from your childhood, for example, Children are to be seen and not heard. or If you want anything done right, you have to do it yourself.
- Place a checkmark beside any of those listed above that you adopted and would now like to unlearn and replace.
- For each statement checked above, write an alternative belief/ thought that represents your thinking now based on your values as an adult, for example, I don t have to do it by myself it is okay to ask someone for help.
- When you think or hear yourself saying the old beliefs/ thoughts, correct them with the new ones you listed. It takes awareness and practice to change a long-held belief. Write these on sticky notes and place them where you will see them daily.

If you are having trouble identifying your old beliefs, ask a friend for help.

Write what your life looks like when you release these old beliefs and adopt new ones.

Emotional Well-Being

Knowing how to take care of your mind and your emotional well-being are essential parts of safeguarding your overall wellness. Most people think about their health and only consider healthy lifestyle choices such as diet, nutrition, and exercise. However, your psychological fitness is just as necessary as your physical health, and when you take care of one of these, you help to take care of the other. Meditation, controlling your stress level, and emotional well-being are also important topics to discuss with your doctor when you visit them next time.

Today, many people in our society consider emotional health as unimportant in their lives. Some even believe that getting in touch with their emotions is a sign of weakness that they should not show to others. Others feel constant pressure all the time to seem happy, to put only their most positive emotions out there for others to see. Just look at social media, where it has become the norm to share your joy and joyful news but rarely, if ever, to acknowledge the struggles in your life.

When we only show others our best selves or celebrate the wins rather than looking for support for the losses, we are doing ourselves and others a real disservice. However, showing emotions to other people is not managing, expressing, or controlling your emotions. Emotional health is a multi-dimensional process that requires many skills and affects our health in significant ways.

What is Emotional Health?

As stated earlier, your emotions dictate how you feel and act throughout the day. As much as we believe we are rational thinking beings, it is our emotions and the way we feel that are responsible for the way we act and interact with others. That is why taking care of our emotional health is so important, especially for spiritual growth.

People who maintain their emotional health have control over their feelings, thoughts, and behaviors and cope better with life's challenges. They find it easier to keep problems in perspective and don't struggle to bounce back after running into an obstacle. They have great relationships with others and high self-confidence.

However, that does not mean emotionally healthy people are constantly happy. They are simply aware of their emotions. They can manage them, whether it s a negative emotion or a positive one. When you are emotionally healthy, you will still experience the gamut of emotions, and you will still get stressed out at times. It isn't a magical cure-all; it's simply that you can deal with your emotions. Emotionally healthy individuals also recognize when a problem is too great to tackle on their own.

Maintaining your emotional health will assist you to cope with stress and work more productively, which will help you contribute to society and to work with others.

Factors Affecting Your Emotional Health

Many factors affect your emotional well-being. Physical ailments, beliefs and values, what you eat, heavy drinking, or abuse of drugs influence your mind. How you handle stress and changes in your life also affect your emotional well-being. Here are a few common influences on your emotional health.

- Getting laid off or losing your job
- Receiving a promotion or changing jobs
- Getting married or divorced
- Becoming injured or having a serious illness
- Caring for a loved one that is injured or ill
- When a child leaves or returns home
- Having or adopting a child
- Dealing with the death of someone you love
- Moving to a new city or home
- Financial difficulties

Looking After Your Emotional Health

If your mental state is causing physical symptoms and you feel you are unable or unwilling to take care of your healthcare needs, or if your emotional symptoms interfere with your life, talk with your doctor or mental health professional.

Your primary care physician should routinely get some information about your feelings and emotions in the same way they monitor other physical symptoms. Let your doctor know if you have feelings of uneasiness, stress, depression, or unable to manage your emotions. Being honest with yourself and your doctor will empower you to adapt to whatever you are facing in your life.

Along with medications and psychological treatment, there are various habits, techniques, and strategies that you can use to boost your emotional well-being.

Warning Signs of Poor Emotional Health

Here are a few warning signs that your emotional health may be suffering.

1. You Argue a Lot

It's normal to have disagreements or arguments, but when you are not managing your emotions well, these disagreements will happen more often. If you find yourself arguing a lot with loved ones, co-workers, strangers, or friends, your emotional health suffers. You are likely not reading or understanding other people s emotions, struggling to understand your own sources of anger, or caught in a perpetual cycle of negative emotions.

2. You are not listening to Others Perspectives

People who cannot manage their emotions often feel like they are always right, and others are wrong, even before they hear what others might say. Neglecting to consider the emotions of others and being critical without hearing their side is a sign that your emotions are out of balance.

3. You Are Living in Denial

Believing that everything in your life is great while having evidence to the contrary is a sign of poor emotional health. Denial of troublesome feelings is not an effective way to cope with or manage these emotions, and eventually, it will harm you and others. When you deny that there might be a problem when others or the facts tell you otherwise, you are in trouble.

4. You Bully Others

Using bullying to control other people shows that you are making up for a lack of self-worth or confidence by making others feel bad. It is a clear sign that you are in trouble and need to focus on your emotional well-being. If sometimes you are using ridicule, threats, or force to coerce other people into action, then you need to examine your emotional health.

5. You Can't Understand Others Feelings

Do you walk around all day asking, What is WRONG with people? If so, you may lack emotional awareness and control. When you cannot understand why other people are angry, sad, irritated, or even happy, it can lead to miscommunication, annoyance, arguments, and many other negative encounters.

Many people struggle to comprehend other people's emotions, making it even more crucial that you work on developing this skill and regularly practice it.

6.   You Withdraw from Others

If you find you would always rather be alone than with others, chances are, you are not dealing well with your emotions.

You could withdraw due to shame, feeling overwhelmed, not having the energy to deal with others needs, insecurity, or depression. When you isolate yourself, you can create even more emotional problems, including distortions in your thinking and loneliness.

7.   Blaming Other People

If your usual first response is to blame other people for whatever problems arise or to refuse to take responsibility for how they are affecting other people, it could be a sign that you lack awareness of how your emotions are affecting others and leading to problems.

8.   You Are Harming Yourself

Inflicting harm on yourself is a sign that you control emotional pain by influencing physical punishment upon yourself. Self-harm can include anything from starving yourself, cutting, binge eating, reckless behavior, or anything else that puts your health and safety at risk. Harming yourself is a clear sign you are not handling your emotions and may need support to help you get them under control.

9.   Difficulty dealing with Other s Strong Feelings

Instinctively walk (or run) away when someone gets upset shows your emotional health needs work. This avoidance behavior does not allow you to understand other people or learn how to handle your own powerful feelings, either.

10. Using or Abusing Substances

Do you use drugs, alcohol, or other substances to help you get through intense emotions? If, yes it means that you are not dealing with these feelings effectively. Alcohol and drugs are often used to numb your pain or help you forget. Instead of relying on drugs or alcohol to help you manage your emotions, it is much healthier to learn to cope in healthier, more productive ways.

11. You Have Trouble Maintaining Relationships.

Low emotional health can affect your ability to connect with, feel close to friends, family, or partners, and bond with other people. When you are emotionally unhealthy, you may struggle to understand how others feel, meaning they stop trusting you or looking for your companionship.

Even just one or two of the above shows you need to pay attention to developing your emotional wellness. You may tackle this on your own, or you may wish to seek the advice of a professional who can help you devise strategies for changing these negative behaviors.

7 traits Of Emotional Health

Let us now look at what emotionally healthy people look like.

Emotionally healthy people have several common characteristics and habits that allow them to understand and manage their own emotions. Given below are the most common of those characteristics.

1. Self-Awareness

Self-awareness is crucial for managing emotions. It includes not only how you view yourself but also how you think others see you. People who are more self-aware understand themselves better and how their emotions are influencing them. They consider others perceptions of them, are open to honest feedback, and engage in regular introspection.

2. Empathetic

Having empathy allows you to place yourself in someone else s position and understand what they feel from that frame of reference. Empathy allows you to identify and understand how someone else feels, connect to others, and feel for them when they are struggling or when they are happy.

3. Adaptable

Adaptability allows you to respond to situations as they present themselves and makes you more resilient to the obstacles and setbacks that are inevitable in life. It enables you to choose a new path when your current one keeps you from experiencing genuine happiness. Emotionally healthy individuals can recognize when they need to stick to their planned course and when they need to switch lanes.

4.   Optimistic

You are more likely to enjoy positive outcomes and stronger emotional health when you are optimistic. Having positive thoughts about the future is important for your emotional health. It allows you to seek solutions when problems arise, overcome difficulties, and set higher goals than if you were pessimistic.

5.   Having faith

Believing that life is happening for you and not to you helps you have self-control over your life and actions. Believing in yourself and your ability to control and regulate your life is essential for emotional health and growth.

6.   Curious

Curiosity means that you are open to improvement and continuous learning, which can help you in the long run to maintain emotional health. Curiosity enables you to grow and strive to be your best, ask yourself questions about the world, and understand other's perspectives.

7.   Analytical

Being able to take in, process, and analyze information will allow you to use your reason and logic more than your emotions to make crucial decisions in your life. When you are analytical, you can examine old habits, perspectives, or behaviors to determine if they are still helping to improve your life. Having an analytical mind enables you to consider the why of your existence, which grounds you and allows you to be passionate about the values and beliefs that guide your life.

8.   Discerning

Knowing the difference between your needs and your wants allows you to make more healthy, informed choices. Emotionally healthy people can tell the difference between their personal needs and wants.

How to Improve Your Health and Well-being

There are many ways to achieve improved health and well-being. However, it starts with setting your well-being as a priority. Below, we will explore the different ways you can take to improve your overall emotional and physical health, and in almost all these exercises or habits, you will see how improving one of these two aspects of wellness will influence the other.

Select those who will help you restore the balance to your life, whatever that may be. Work to make it a regular part of your routine and include it in your life as much as possible or as you need.

Learn to Express Your Feelings

When you experience powerful emotions, you need to learn how to express them appropriately, which allows you to release them and find productive ways to move forward. If you choose not to express your emotions, you can end up having internal stress. This can make you feel even worse than you do from your initial feelings. Pent-up feelings of stress, anxiety, anger, or sadness can lead to further emotional turmoil and physical symptoms.

Some people fear that expressing their emotions means losing control of their emotional self, but in reality, communicating is the healthier choice. You will still feel the emotions when you express them.

Expressing your feelings allows you to talk about and show what is bothering you, which is the first step to finding a productive solution to moving forward. Letting others know what is bothering you also communicates your boundaries and needs, showing others how they can help you.

When you share your problems with others, it gives you the chance to get feedback or another perspective from others, which can help you view your situation differently.

Identifying what you are feeling and the cause of your feelings can help you figure out triggers that assist you in identifying areas in which you need to focus and find paths forward that help you increase your happiness and success.

Understand Your Values

Remember our beliefs and values help structure our feelings and emotions. Everything we value has an emotional state attached to it. Therefore, we must look at our values and see how well they are serving our needs. The first step in discovering what you value most in life is making a list of the essential things you value. Think about the emotional comfort you feel from having this value. For example, if you value money, what would be the feeling of having a lot of money? Is it comfort, Joy, or freedom?

Clarify the feeling you want to experience rather than the material things or achievements that would give you that feeling. Make a list of ten feelings you value most in life (integrity, honesty, love, trust, freedom, commitment, etc.).

Discover your Rules

We all live by conscious and unconscious rules. However, most people live their entire life responding to rules without being conscious of them. Unspoken rules can harm a relationship as we can feel hurt or disappointed when others violate our subconscious rule.

I had a client whose subconscious rule was that her husband should always kiss her every morning as he was leaving for work. On days that he did not, she felt hurt and disappointed, wondering what was wrong. The husband was not aware that this was a rule, as it was not something that they spoke or agreed on. He just spontaneously did it, or she would, in the beginning, ask him for a kiss when he left.

Rules are the way we organize the feelings that are most important to us. Your rules can limit your interaction with others. Understanding your rules will help you understand why you do what you do. It will help you clarify the feelings and emotions you want to have. Without consciously and intelligently organizing your rules, they will create barriers that prevent you from feeling what you want to feel. Revisit your top values and rewrite your rules to experience your top values consistently.

Seek Balance in Your Life

Wellness is about achieving a balance between all the various aspects of your life. When you focus too much on one component, it leaves you with no energy or ability to focus on other critical areas. When you obsess over a specific problem or give all your energy to work, family, or leisure activities, you neglect the other parts of your life necessary for real well-being.

Over time, your priorities will shift, and certain things in your life will be more critical than others, but it is still essential that you determine what balance is best for you to always devote some time to all aspects of your wellness.

So, while your career may be necessary when you are younger and less critical when you are in your mid-years, it is still essential during these times that you devote energy to the other and to the many aspects that comprise a full and happy life.

Become More Resilient

When you have resilience, you can cope with stress and keep yourself healthy. Resilience allows you to overcome limitations and get better from setbacks while also choosing to align with what you accept as true and important in life.

Resilience is a skill that you can learn or develop, and it is essential for emotional health and physical well-being. You can learn to become more resilient with practice and by engaging in specific training activities.

To develop resilience, focus on creating and maintaining a healthy support system. Keeping an optimistic outlook and maintaining a positive view of yourself is also essential.

Learning to accept change and keep setbacks or failures in perspective is also vital.

Engage in Mind and Body Calming Activities

Self-awareness and relaxation strategies can help you calm your mind and body, improving your emotional and physical health. Effective mind-body techniques include Transcendental Meditation using guided imagery, yoga, tai chi, introspection and self-awareness, and deep-breathing. These activities bring your attention to your present reality, calm your heart rate and release tension and stress you may be feeling more about this in the following chapters.

Eat A Healthier Diet

Eating a diet filled with healthy, natural foods rich in nutrients will help give your mind and body the fuel it needs while eliminating harmful additives that can influence your physical and mental well-being.

Your diet influences your body, and when you load it with healthy ingredients that contain the right amounts of fat, carbohydrates, and protein, it will respond by keeping you healthy and giving you the energy you need to live your life. When you neglect your diet, your body will respond with physical and emotional symptoms.

Exercise

Regular exercise allows your body to regulate the hormones that help regulate mood. It also strengthens your muscles, including your heart, helps improve your mood, enhances your brain function, and improves how your body functions.

Activity release neurotransmitters that help boost your outlook, and when you exercise outdoors, you will enjoy additional mental and emotional benefits.

Get the right medical care

Your primary care provider should not only be interested in your physical but also in your mental health, and you should feel comfortable talking with him or her about your emotional pain and any physical issues you may be having.

If you are struggling with your emotional or mental state, then enlisting the advice and support of a mental health professional could also be helpful. Seek the help you need and always talk honestly and openly with those entrusted with your care.

Overcome the Brain's Instinct for Negative Thinking

The more stressed and unhealthier you are, the greater the tendency to think negatively. In survival situations, this enables you to remain vigilant and avoid danger or threats. But, in everyday life, a constant focus on what is wrong or bad in our lives is not productive. This negativity bias keeps you dwelling on past mistakes or problems or gets you so upset over minor frustrations in your day.

Instead of allowing your mind to focus on this negativity, you need to focus on retraining your brain to look instead at what is positive and enjoyable in your life.

Improve your attitude

Your outlook is one part of your emotional health that you can control each day. When negative things happen, or you feel negative emotions creeping in, turn those into positive thoughts. This will also help you become more resilient. Focus on the positive aspects of the situation, look for ways to learn from mistakes or missteps, and focus on what is important to you for your future. If you keep in mind that situations occurring in your life help you grow, it will be easier to see how even the adverse conditions help you on your path.

Focus on gratitude, being mindful of how negative thoughts are influencing you, and learning to experience the world with wonder can keep you from focusing on the negative.

A simple technique to control negative self-directed thoughts, for example saying I am stupid, when you make a mistake, is to wear a rubberband on your wrist. Every time you have a negative self-directed thought, you snap the band. This will create a physical sensation that will remind you that you should think in a more positive way about yourself. If you do this for a day you will be surprised how many negative thoughts you have about yourself each day. Try this exercise for a week. Remember to snap the rubberband every time you have a negative thought, and replace it with a positive thought.

This simple activity will retrain your mind to think positively.

Learn to Forgive

If you walk around harboring resentment or other negative emotions toward another, you are much more likely to have health problems and suffer from other emotional and psychological issues.

Forgiveness, which is the act of acceptance regarding an event and letting go of your negative feelings about what happened, helps you experience more positive physical and mental health.

Forgiveness does not mean that you have forgotten what has happened, but you accept it is over. You no longer wish to feel bad about it, and you can take the lessons you learned and use them to inform your future.

Learning to forgive can boost your immune system and even help you live longer. Harboring ill will or bad feelings can have a negative impact on your heart and overall health, so learn to let go and move on.

When you learn to forgive others or even yourself, you will notice that you feel less pain, you are not easily angered, and that some physical symptoms you may have been feeling have resolved.

Guard your self-esteem.

Learning to feel confident and comfortable with yourself is an essential habit of protecting your emotional wellness and safeguarding your well-being. High self-esteem makes you less critical of yourself, and others actions or words are less likely to affect you. Being compassionate towards yourself protects your self-esteem and provides you with more protection from emotional dysfunction.

Learn to handle failure

Instead of looking at failure as something negative, it is better for your emotional health to take control of your reactions and turn failure into a positive. Look at failure as an opportunity to examine what you need to do to succeed in the future and move forward with a more informed plan. Using failure as feedback helps you identify the factors you can control and allows you to take control of your motivation and plans.

Be realistic

Having unrealistic expectations can set you up for failure, lower your self-esteem when things do not turn out well, and can, over time, lead to diminished emotional health. When you keep your expectations for yourself and other people more realistic, you are more likely to be happier, enjoy better outcomes, and learn more from your experiences.

Be your best friend

Treat yourself as you would do with a cherished friend, including how you talk to yourself and the expectations you have for your abilities and outcome. Be gentle with yourself about your imperfections in the same way you would about your best friends or partners. Treat yourself with kindness, understanding, and forgiveness.

Decrease your stress level

Under stress, we become more reactive. Stress also creates biochemical changes that can be harmful to your health. Research has proven Transcendental Meditation to release stress and create balance in health. Meditation, exercise, and finding enjoyable activities can help you cope with stress in your life.[6]

Practice Deep Breathing

Taking deep breaths is an effective way to reduce stress, release tension in your body, and calm your mind. People who practice deep breathing regularly notice improvements in their ability to think and reason and having lower blood pressure.

Taking deep breaths with your attention on your breath allows you to block out negative emotions and center your thoughts on something other than anxiety or stress. Learning to breathe deeply can have a positive influence on your life and your health.

Set goals and work to achieve them

Having a sense of purpose is very helpful for maintaining motivation in life, and when you set realistic and attainable goals for yourself, then work to achieve them, you will enjoy a sense of accomplishment. Working toward goals can help build your self-esteem and the trust you have in yourself. Get enough quality sleep.

A good night's sleep is vital for your physical and your mental health. Lack of sleep causes tiredness and affects your ability to cope with stress, recognize and manage your emotions, and focus. Make sure you are not only getting enough sleep but that your rest is quality. Develop a sleep routine that works for you and stick to it, no matter what.

---

[6]   Scientific Research on Maharishi s Transcendental Meditation Program: Collected Papers, Volume 4: 2245-2266, 1989

Build strong connections to others.

Having strong and healthy relationships can improve your emotional and physical health. Relationships can come from many sources and do not have to be romantic to be significant to your emotional well-being. Having a wide circle of friends and people you can rely on will keep you healthier and happier throughout your life.

Stop brooding

Brooding over things that have already happened affects your mood and motivation. If bad things happen in your life, it is essential to process those emotions and then move on. Change your thoughts to something more positive as soon as those ruminating thoughts creep in and stop dwelling on things you cannot control if you want to enjoy emotional well-being.

Honor your boundaries.

Having strong emotional health allows you to know when to set boundaries that honor your wellness and how to keep others from disregarding those boundaries. Setting boundaries can help keep you healthy and allow you to honor what is necessary for you, but it requires courage and self-esteem to ensure that others honor those boundaries, as well.

Learn to deal with loss.

Whether it is a death, the end of a relationship, losing a job, or some other disappointment in your life, learning to deal with loss is an integral part of emotional well-being. Learning to mourn your loss, acknowledge and confront your feelings, and then move on is an essential part of emotional well-being.

Learn to Say no.

Taking care of yourself and respecting your time and needs is also crucial. When you say yes to everyone else, it leaves very little time for you. Saying no is a combination of self-care and setting boundaries and allows you the time you need to take care of what is important to you. Overextending yourself leads to stress and an inability to cope with other emotions, so know when to say enough.

Be responsible for yourself

Accepting responsibility for your emotions, behavior, and all that you do to influence your existence puts you in charge of your life. Giving over responsibility to others or blaming them for your situation is a sign that you have not accepted responsibility and allow others to dictate your emotional well-being. Remember, only you can make yourself happy.

Value personal development

Emotionally healthy people understand the value of personal growth and development. They seek advice from others, search for new opportunities to learn, and focus on ways to better themselves and their lives.

Practice self-awareness

When you learn to be more self-aware, you become more conscious of what is happening around you and how it affects you. Those who regularly engage in self-awareness practices are more likely to be more aware of their emotions and live a more purposeful life.

Self-awareness is a continuous work in action. It is not a one-time job. We have to work diligently on our inner development to unfold the total value and gifts that we are and can offer the world. The more self-aware you become, the happier and more fulfilled you will be. Self-awareness, in its absolute sense, means being aware of your true nature, your inner being, the Self. The Self is beyond the body and mind. It is the soul of our being. It is the source of all the energy, intelligence, peace, love, and happiness that we seek in outer life. When we lose connection with our source, we suffer, become unhappy, unhealthy, and lack fulfillment in life. We may become financially successful but will never feel completely satisfied or fulfilled. The Self is your connection to the Divine within. To know that is to go beyond (transcend) the constant chatter or your mind into the silence of your own being.

Know when to get help

Being emotionally healthy does not mean having all the answers or being perfect. Instead, it means knowing that sometimes you may need the support of others to cope with some of your emotions. Getting help from a support network or a professional is all healthy signs that you value your emotional help and do what it takes to accomplish that goal.

Sign up with a coach

A coach will assist you in overcoming the health and emotional problems you may be facing. The personal benefits of coaching vary depending on the individuals involved. Many people report that coaching positively impacted their careers and their lives by helping them to:

- Establish and take action towards achieving goals
- Become more self-reliant
- Gain more job and life satisfaction
- Contribute more effectively to the team and the organization
- Take greater responsibility and accountability for actions and commitments
- Work more efficiently and productively with others (boss, direct reports, peers)
- Communicate more effectively

As a health and life coach, I have helped many people overcome personal challenges. My book, Master Your Emotions-Transform Your Life, contains many valuable exercises to assist you. I have also created the Master Your Emotions–Transform Your Life online course that can help you overcome personal challenges. Visit www.psychedonlife.net for more information.

As stated previously, emotional health is one of the most overlooked sides of your overall well-being, which plays a vital role in your physical health, spiritual development, and overall happiness. Understanding your emotions and learning how to master them is the second most crucial step, after meditation, for anyone who wants to have control over their lives and to gain the understanding necessary for evolution and spiritual growth.

Introspection, practicing self-awareness, and deciding that controlling your emotions is essential to you will all help you achieve emotional health.

CHAPTER 5

Intellect

The intellect comprises many parts. We have seen in the previous chapters that the finest aspects of the intellect are, first, the awareness of I am " the self, next is the feeling and emotions, and the last level is the conscious thinking level where we have thoughts. On this level, we analyze, discriminate, and decide on our feelings, emotions, and information gained from our environment and senses.

It is the nature of the intellect to discriminate, to take the wholeness and break it up into parts so we can have a greater understanding of ourselves, our environment, and the world. This is how we gain knowledge.

Knowledge is power. The more we act on the knowledge we have about the Self, the more control we will have over our life. To have actual knowledge, we need to have intellectual understanding and direct experience. Intellectual understanding without direct personal experience will not allow us to live the knowledge we gain.

Many understand the philosophy of life, spirituality, and self-realization, but without the direct experience of this level of reality, they cannot live it. Unfortunately, this is the faith of most of the education offered today. For example, many people with degrees in psychology and sociology still cannot effectively handle their personal life and relationships. Some physicians knowing that smoking, excessive drinking, and processed foods are not suitable for your health, will still overindulge. It is not important just to know what is right; we have to live what is right. When we learn to ride a bike, we effortlessly perform that activity without thinking because knowledge has become part of us. It is ingrained in our physiology. The knowledge is no longer theoretical; we live the knowledge. This is how all knowledge that is useful to life should be.

Thoughts

Thoughts are vibrating energy. Our intention and attention cause thought to express itself in a particular direction; our feelings and emotions are the finest expressions of thought.

It is now a fact that our thoughts create chemical reactions in our bodies. Negative thoughts increase stress hormones such as cortisol, adrenaline and can lead to serious illness. Therefore, it is crucial to know how to reduce negative thoughts and have more positive thoughts in our life. The practice of introspection and self-awareness allows us to do just that with our life.

Meditation allows us to become aware of the Self. In meditation, we turn our attention within to experience finer states of the thinking process until the mind experiences the finest state, arriving at the source of the thinking process, the Self, which is the home of all knowledge. This inner experience broadens our awareness to understand and appreciate the subtler levels of creation and the more expressed levels of relative life.

Introspection and Self-Awareness

Over the years, my circumstances forced me to take a deep look at my life, where I am, and where I want to be. My periods of introspection have helped me to become more aware of myself. Introspection and Self-awareness have two aspects. One is where we turn the attention inward during meditation; the other is when we analyze our behavior, thoughts, and actions.

They are both necessary for growth. I continue to practice both regularly.

How Self-Aware Are You?

Self-awareness begins with introspection and self-reflection. It is a process, a journey you walk through life.

To be self-aware is to have a greater understanding of who you are, what your weaknesses and strengths are, what helped shape you, and how your behavior (or even just your presence) impacts others.

Self-awareness and emotional intelligence go hand-in-hand. People with high levels of emotional intelligence also have high levels of self-awareness. Self-awareness and emotional intelligence are now two popular traits with potential employers. Of course, they are also essential traits to have for potential romantic relationships.

Personal Growth

Introspection allows you to tap into all those things that promote or stop you from becoming your best self. Through introspection, meditation, and subsequent self-awareness, you enhance your mental, emotional, and spiritual growth. Without introspection, there can be no self-actualization. According to Maslow's Hierarchy of Needs, self-realization is the realization or fulfillment of one's talents, and potentialities considered a drive or need present in everyone.

With introspection, you discover all the negative patterns in your life that stop you from being your best and living your best life. This knowledge facilitates the ultimate opportunities for personal growth and development. Without introspection, the growth and development you seek are not possible.

Introspection allows you to gain a wealth of self-awareness and self-understanding. Through self-awareness and self-understanding, you open a variety of doors, including identifying your desires, values, and the life which makes you most content.

It's important that you understand what happens when you lack self-awareness, that you know how to correct it, and that you know what that looks like after the fact. Look at the following and see how they apply to you.

Micromanager

Are you a micromanager? If so, you most likely have a good reason, as most micromanagers are perfectionists at heart. Or perhaps you're micromanaging because this is your first time leading a major project, and it all rests on you. Or maybe you're dealing with someone you know needs motivation. Those seem like valid reasons to micromanage, don't they?

There's just one thing missing a greater understanding of how your need to take control affects others. When you micromanage, you demoralize. You signal to others that you don't trust them, whether it's a point-by-point list for your spouse or you hover behind people at work. You make assumptions about others and tear them down.

So, how can you be more self-aware in this situation? You can start by recognizing that you do not exist in a vacuum, and you need to work on trusting others. Remember, you're working toward the same goal.

Faultless

How often do you look for a way to lay blame elsewhere? Something has gone wrong. You played a role in it, but you have a better fall guy, so you walk away squeaky clean.

If your response to critique, criticism, or feedback is yeah, but then the reality is you're looking for a way to deflect negative attention you don't want. It's an understandable response, but have you ever thought about how that looks to others? They could think that you are someone who avoids accountability. You could appear to be dismissive.

How do you overcome this type of habit? You need the awareness to see how people react to how you express your feelings and opinions. It's related to emotional intelligence in that you learn to separate your own thoughts from the observations you make of others' behavior.

When you slip up, take accountability. People respond positively when you acknowledge your mistakes instead of trying to blame others.

Defensive

Are you angry or upset when someone offers feedback? Do you view all feedback as unwarranted, harsh, or unexpected criticism? Are negative emotions swirling within you when a colleague critiques you? Try to figure out why that upsets you so much. A bit of self-reflection will let you know the reason.

Feedback is a normal part of life, whether it's at work or home. Most feedback helps you grow. It isn't always personal, even if it might feel as though it is. Nobody is perfect and growth matters. It won't be easy to accept, and you will feel anxious in the face of unexpected criticism. It s natural. However, it will help you identify areas ready for growth.

Careless Words

Wouldn't life be easier if everyone could just read your mind to know that you're hurt, angry, frustrated, upset, or sad? It would certainly be easier than trying to express your feelings. It's safer to say I'm fine when you are not, in fact, fine. We want people to view us as confident, competent, and capable, and the best way to avoid confrontation and deflect emotions is through passive-aggressive behavior.

When you are careless with your words or engage in passive-aggressive behavior to communicate, then you're guilty of two things. One of them is the initial behavior and the other one is setting unrealistic expectations for the people around you; they are not mind-readers, no matter how much you'd like them to be.

You're also exhausting everyone involved, including yourself. When you're dealing with powerful emotions, always take a moment before you respond. As tempting as it is to bottle up your issues, you must find a way to express them evenly. It's a delicate balance.

Humorless

Many people struggle with a fear of embarrassment. No one enjoys feeling embarrassed, and for many, it evokes feelings of shame. When you realize you're the butt of the joke, laughing is the last thing on your mind. Instead of laughing it off, you get angry and lash out at the people around you. Instead of sitting with the discomfort, you distract yourself by deflecting.

Self-awareness means accepting that you're upset, ashamed, or embarrassed and laughing about it, anyway. It might sound like a small thing, but when you can laugh at yourself, it shows that you are aware you can make mistakes and have accepted that it's something that happens sometimes. It's not that deep.

You're Not Listening

Are you a good listener? If your answer is yes, I encourage you to ask why you believe that to be true.

Think about this. You had been working on a project you finished just in time to meet the deadline. You felt nervous about your work. There were some other bits and pieces that you would have liked to include, but you didn't have time. You did have an idea that could strengthen the overall response, but it was too late. Despite all those nerves, your presentation got great feedback. Everyone responded positively, except for one person.

In this situation, who did you choose to listen to? Did you focus on all the positive responses? Or did you dwell on the person who didn't respond positively? Perhaps it is the latter, which means you aren't actually listening, are you? You dwell on the response that got you in your feelings, confirming your insecurities. Is this something you often do?

Do you think about what you're going to say and wait until someone stops speaking so you can jump in and say your piece? If that's what you do, are you listening?

When communicating, listening is vital. That isn't some major secret, but it isn't easy. It's what and how you listen that matters. Self-awareness means listening, not listening for. Listen to everything they have to say, not just the parts you want to hear.

Making Changes

Introspection provides you with the opportunity to change those things about yourself that are causing you unhappiness and dysfunction in your life. An honest exploration of self provides the knowledge needed to make any changes that do not serve you.

Key Questions

Have you ever wondered, why did I do that or why do I keep doing this ? Becoming self-aware through introspection can answer these questions and open a variety of doors in self-discovery.

As you reflect on all the different versions of yourself, you will also reflect on the current version of yourself. This will help you get a deeper insight into the future you. What is the best version of yourself?

You might find old qualities you would like to reconnect with. Or you realized you're negative now because you've been holding onto years of negative emotions. Either way, through introspection, you learn everything there is to know about you. Introspection provides access to your true inner self to achieve the highest level of self-understanding.

CHAPTER 6

Introspection

It is really important to take some time out regularly for introspection. I recommend that at least every four months, take some time off to do some introspection and to re-evaluate your life goals and aspirations. This will help you see if you are heading in the right direction with your life. With introspection, you can find answers to crucial questions " What do I do? And most important: Why Do I Do This? For example,

- Why do I feel angry all the time?
- Why can't I keep a relationship for more than four months?
- Why do I keep attracting the wrong partner? Why do I struggle with relationships?
- Why do I put others ahead of me?
- Why can't I stand up for myself?
- What stops me from achieving my goals?
- I hate my job, why can't I leave it?
- And many others.

Introspection can provide answers to such questions and allow you to gain a great deal of personal knowledge. It provides knowledge that is not possible to get in any other way and allows to make important connections that then are used to make critical changes.

It helps you appreciate who you are

It's much easier to get a sense of where you are now when you realize all the places you have been. Not only will you have a greater appreciation of who you are today, but you will also have a greater understanding of just how far you have come.

Creates Gratitude

While it's normal for humans to fear change, the reality of the matter is that change is not always bad. We tend to focus on negative changes and conveniently overlook the small things that make positive differences. Introspection helps you get a better hold on this, which makes you a more grateful person.

Leads to Forgiveness

As you reflect on your past, you will, sometimes, remember some missteps you have made in your life. It will drag up all the mistakes you made, the conversations you walked away from wishing you'd said this or that. It's cringe-worthy, and it would be so much better if you could just forget it ever happened. However, with self-reflection comes self-growth. Forgiveness plays a large part in this process as you learn to cut yourself some slack.

Brings Clarity

As you sit and connect the dots between who you are now versus your past experiences, you gain clarity over why you are the person you are. This can be useful for reinforcing qualities you'd like to keep and the ones you'd like to purge if you have a history of poor relationships. This will continue until you get to the root of why. Maybe your first relationship was poor and every version of you tries to fix it with every new relationship, but it just exacerbates the cycle.

It's A Connection

You might find old qualities and traits you deemed negative or harmful. The benefit of hindsight might just highlight the positive aspects of those qualities. Perhaps it's time for you to reconnect with that part of your past self.

We are sometimes guilty of disposing of traits and qualities that we deem bad because someone else insinuates it's a negative trait or quality. Or we blame that specific quality or trait for the outcome. By practicing self-reflection and by taking time out for introspection, you get a much greater view of how those traits contributed to the experience you had.

Improves Self-Esteem

It's much easier to build your self-esteem and feel better about yourself if you appreciate the entirety of your journey. You aren't who you are because of the big moments. You are just as shaped by the insignificant moments. A lot went into shaping you as the person you are now, and it should help you come to grips with some of your mistakes and errors.

The Emotional Release

The experiences you had long forgotten or stopped thinking about years ago, you will remember them as you skim through your memory.

When you do, you will relive all the emotions you experienced. Those emotions never went away but have been beneath the surface all this time. Introspection will eventually help you put those emotions to rest.

Make Better Decisions

Through introspection, self-understanding, and awareness, you get very close to your desires, needs, and conscience. This helps you make much better decisions for anything in life.

Build Character

Look inside with honesty and thoroughness to confront the person you are. You will find out all those things that make you who you are, the good and the bad, what you believe in, and what you have done and not done. This takes strength and resolve and therefore builds character as you go through the journey of self-discovery.

Block Out External influences

You can focus on yourself through introspection. By blocking out the external influences you have in life, such as family, friends, and society, and focusing on yourself, you allow yourself the opportunity to live your own way and make changes based on your own conscience. This ensures that you take responsibility for your own life.

Acknowledgment of Choices

Self-awareness presents you with an abundance of choices so you can design your greatest self and your greatest life.

Improved Self-Control and Self-Regulation

Self-awareness promotes self-control and improves self-regulation. Understanding yourself and why you do what you do or react in certain ways allows you to keep what you need and change the rest.

Liberate Yourself

Introspection helps you understand your own responsibility in life. When you become accountable for your behaviors, thoughts, and feelings, you reduce stress, gain peace of mind, and have more control over your life.

Gain Empathy

When you understand yourself, you are much better at underrating others. This type of empathy makes you a better person in all your relationships. You become more supportive, caring, and giving to others, making you a better you overall and better at navigating the world.

Change Perceptions

When you understand yourself, you will learn what perceptions you can carry with you in life. Our own perceptions mainly dictate how you react and act in all facets of your life.

For example, if your parents beat you as a child and you believed you deserved it, your perception of yourself is that you do not deserve love or caring from anyone as an adult. This perception may dictate who you attract in your life, and the relationships you engage in might support this perception that you carry.

When you reflect and realize this, you can then explore that this perception is flawed and that you are not bad; it was the abuser who was bad. You can change your perception of yourself and understand that you are good, and you deserve supportive and caring relationships in your life.

Retake Real Control

Through introspection, you can detach yourself from all those things in life for which you have no control. Instead, you direct your energy on yourself and self-improvement.

Take Action

Introspection is a process, whether you want to uncover your passion, purpose, or you just need clarity on a specific issue that's bothering you. Inner work is never easy, but it's necessary if you want to move forward and progress on the right path for your life. Introspection is sitting back and taking in your inner world to figure out what's going on. Following a period of introspection, after observing your inner-world and analyzing it, your next step is to decide what you want to do about it. Analysis without action is empty.

A client of mine was having some relationship problems, and I suggested that he spend some time introspecting. In our follow-up session, he revealed he realized what the problem was. I asked him to continue the process of introspection, asking a series of whys. As he continued the process, he discovered deeper issues stemming from his childhood and relationship with his parents. Through continued introspection, he found that there were more factors involved than he was initially aware of.

This is something we're all guilty of. We introspect and believe we have it nailed. However, we usually seize on the first reason our brain finds and go with it. Having uncovered the many issues he had regarding his relationships, we talked it out, and through a series of exercises, he was able to take action to resolve them.

The important part of the process was when we figured out the action to take. We addressed the actions that he could take to clear his decks and settle the issues once and for all. This allowed him to improve his relationships.

Deep introspection helps you gain self-awareness and understand what you do, why you do it, how you feel, your beliefs, mindsets, and who you are. There is no better way to get to the root of an issue. However, you can't stop there. There is more work to do.

While the introspection aspect is key to self-awareness, it isn't enough. If you stop there, you won't get the benefit of introspection. The payoff doesn't come until you identify what action you can take to make the proper changes.

Dissatisfaction, unhappiness, and struggles are all signs that something of value is at stake in your life. It needs attention. It is of worth and in need of a rescue mission of some sort. If you want to keep it, then introspection will help you find what action you should take. If it's time to let it go, introspection will also help you find the right action.

Remember, you can't get closure from anything until you take action. Introspection without action is empty, it's hollow, and it's meaningless. Bear this in mind as you observe and analyze your inner self. Every note you make, every thought you have, should create a plan of action.

Once you have done the initial deep-dive introspection, you can make it a regular occurrence. There is a lot less work to do if you frequently check in with yourself. It's always wise to monitor how things are progressing and connect to ensure you're still in harmony.

The introspection process might be a long and frustrating one as you get started, but the good news is that it gets easier the longer you do it. With regular practice, you will reach a point where it's second nature. You won't even think about doing it; it will be your automatic response when you face overwhelming issues or problems in your life.

Here are some questions to get you started.

Answer the following questions. Be thorough, honest, and thoughtful. If you are not sure of the answer, write that down and mark it, you can use it later when you delve deeper into introspection and self-awareness. The goal of this exercise is for you to get deep into introspection and discover who you are on the deepest level.

- What is my purpose, passions, meaning in life?
- What do you believe your strengths to be? Take this opportunity to make a list.
- How could your strengths improve your life and/or help others?
- What do people often tell you you're good at?
- What have you done to help the people around you?
- What brings you happiness?
- What are you naturally good at? What comes easy?
- What subject or topic could you talk about endlessly without realizing it?
- What are my weaknesses?
- What do I dislike about my life?

This is your chance to be honest. If you dislike your job, then be honest about disliking your job. If you dislike how a friend is treating you, be honest about disliking how a friend treats you. You will never understand yourself or fix any problems if you beat around the bush. Once you dig in, you realize that many of the things you do stem from your dislike for specific things, people, or areas of your life.

What is going well in my life?

It's easy to focus on the negative things; there's just something about them that draws our attention. However, positive introspection matters. Pay attention to what is going well in your life. When you are aware of what's going well, it's easier to spot the actual problems where things are going wrong. It's also a great motivator to get you back on track.

You can learn a lot about why you do what you do from what is going well in your life, too. Think about the positive decisions you make when your mood is high?

What has been changing?

Change is constant; it never lets up. Yet daily life can be monotonous. We are busy micro-managing daily routines, and we don't notice all the surrounding changes. Introspection is a wonderful opportunity to consider what has changed in the last week, month, year, and how change has impacted you and why you do what you do.

What inspires you?

Do you have a life mission?

These are just some questions to get you thinking. Of course, you can add your own questions to the list.

The action you take depends on the problem at hand. It is difficult to offer general advice in this area, but here are some key problem-solving options.

- The first step is introspection and gaining self-awareness. Once you have identified the issues you want to work on, you can make a detailed plan to resolve these issues and begin the recovery process. Make a detailed plan on alternatives to replace current behavior patterns. Make a plan to stop your usual cycles, patterns, and habits.

- Start re-programing your mind towards positivity by using visualization, meditation, and positive affirmations.
- You can also enlist the help of a coach. Coaches can help you gain clarity and take action.
- Talk with a therapist and get counseling. This is one of the best options to make significant changes and jump into a healing process.
- Create a strong support system to help you deal with your issues. Talk about your issues and ask for feedback and help from the support system in aiding you, such as letting you know when you slip into old habits.
- Stop blaming and take responsibility for yourself and your life today.
- There are various apps on the internet that help with personal growth, and depending on the issues you are working on, they may be helpful to you.
- Create a vision board. Use magazines and other photo sources to create a board that embodies the goal you are trying to reach. Put it up at home where you can see it often.
- Listen to motivational podcasts every morning.
- Online discussion boards and forums may be helpful. Some online forums have thousands of supportive members and are dealing with the same issues as you. To begin, read through some posts to make sure it is a quality forum.

CHAPTER 7

Pranamayakosha:– Breath and Energy

From the subtler aspects of the feelings, intellect, and mind, we will now consider the grosser aspects of physiology, the breath, and the physical body. We have seen in previous chapters that the body comprises a series of energy fields. When they vibrate in harmony, we experience good health. When there is disruption, we experience discomfort and disease.

Vibrating energy emits sounds we feel and hear. Nature has its own vibration, and when we attune ourselves to nature, we feel contented and happy. That is why spending time in nature, such as taking a walk through the forest, sitting at the seaside, or river, has a soothing effect. Listening to the sounds of birds, the sea, or the wind gently rustling through the trees, can also produce a calming effect on mind and body. Sound vibrations can also be disruptive and can cause chaos and disease in the body.

Researchers at Brighton and Sussex Medical School (BSMS) (University of Sussex, March 2017) found that playing 'natural sounds' affected the bodily systems that control the flight-or-fright and rest-digest autonomic nervous systems, with associated effects in the resting activity of the brain. They noted: When listening to natural sounds, the brain connectivity reflected an outward-directed focus of attention;

when listening to artificial sounds, the brain connectivity reflected an inward-directed focus of attention, similar to states observed in anxiety. (Hett, 29 May 2020)

In his book, Human Physiology Expression of Veda and Vedic Literature, Dr. Tony Nader (Nader, 2000, 2014), explains how human physiology is an expression of the Vedic sounds, mantras, found in the forty aspects of Vedic literature, and how the recitation of these sounds in proper sequence, can enliven the physiology. This discovery opens the possibility to heal the body through the use of Vedic sounds. Vedic vibration technology is now being applied for the treatment of various ailments. Listening to Vedic chanting (without including instruments) can enliven corresponding areas of the body, creating balance and better health.

Chakras

The human physiology has specific channels through which energy flows from its source into the cells and organs of the body. These channels are called chakras. Chakras are the storehouses of energy for the body. There are chakras throughout the physiology. However, the main ones are in the center of the body, from the base of the spine to the top of the head. They are seven in total. The energy in the chakras flows in spirals, similar to a cone. Each has a certain velocity. When the energy in the chakras is restricted, we experience discomfort and disease in mind and body.

The major chakras are the expression of light, each reflecting a particular color of the spectrum of light energy. Every color vibrates at a specific frequency as the sound. Each chakra responds to particular sounds or vibrations. Similarly, the cells and organs of the body are also sound vibrations and respond to specific sounds or vibrations. When the whole physiology is vibrating in harmony, we are healthy. As we increase the vibration in the chakras, we also affect all the cells and organs in the body as each chakra controls the energy in various cells and organs in the physical system and in our other light bodies. This enlivening of the energies in the chakras, organs, and cells change our perception and leads to higher levels of awareness and higher states of consciousness. Rosalyn L Bruyere, an internationally acclaimed healer, clairvoyant, and medicine woman, has written extensively about chakras in her book, Wheels of Light (Bruyere, 1994). It is well worth reading for those interested in learning more about chakras and healing energies.

The first of the main chakras is the root chakra; it is between the spine and the pubic bone. It governs the spinal column, kidneys, and adrenals. The color associated with it is red.

The second chakra is behind and just below the navel, in the sacral area of the body. It governs the reproductive system and the gonads. The color associated with it is orange.

The third chakra is in the V formed by the rib cage, the solar plexus area. It governs the pancreas, stomach, liver, gallbladder, and nervous system. The color associated with it is yellow.

The fourth chakra, also called the heart chakra, is situated midway between the two breasts. It governs the heart, blood, Vagus nerve, circulatory system, and the thymus. The color associated with it is green.

The fifth chakra is in the throat. It governs the bronchial and vocal cord apparatus, lungs, alimentary canal, and thyroid. The color associated with it is blue.

The sixth chakra, also known as the third eye, is between the eyebrows. It governs the lower brain, left eye, ears, nose, nervous system, and pituitary glands. The color associated with it is indigo.

The seventh chakra also referred to as the crown chakra, is at the top of the head. It governs the upper brain, right eye, and the pineal gland. The color associated with it is violet-white. (Brennan, 1988).

Chakras and emotions

1st Chakra (root chakra). This chakra is responsible for your stability and security. When out of balance, you feel fearful and insecure about your life and the things around you.

2nd Charka. It is responsible for your sexuality and creativity. When out of balance, you feel stuck, your creativity doesn t flow, and you might feel unsure of doing and executing plans or projects. You might feel feelings of body shame and sexual guilt.

3rd Chakra (solar plexus chakra). The solar plexus stores a lot of our emotions. Also, sometimes called the bliss chakra, it associated with your self-confidence and inner power. It's connected with your will, and it is the core of your personality, identity, and ego. The imbalance makes you feel powerless, worthless, shameful, rejected, and self-conscious.

4th chakra (heart chakra): It is responsible for the flow of love, spirituality, humanity, and healing. Imbalance in the chakra makes you feel jealous, abandoned, anger, fear, bitterness, rejection, envy, conditional love.

5th chakra (throat chakra): It is responsible for expression, faith, and communication ability. Imbalance of the Throat Chakra may lead to timidity, quietness, a feeling of weakness, or the inability to express your thoughts.

6th Chakra (third eye): It is responsible for intelligence, intuition, understanding, insight, and self-knowledge. When this chakra is out of balance, one might feel non-assertive, afraid of success, or on the contrary, be egoistical.

7th chakra (crown chakra): It is the center of spirituality, enlightenment, dynamic thought, and energy. It allows for the inward flow of wisdom and brings the gift of cosmic consciousness. When out of balance, one might suffer from a constant sense of frustration, no spark of joy, and destructive feelings.

Prana and Qi

In Ayurveda, the flow of life energy or life force is called prana. Qi or Chi in Chinese medicine refers to the same life force. According to Traditional Chinese Medicine (TCM), there are three major sources of QI; breath, food, and constitution.

In Ayurveda, Nadis are the channels through which the energy from the chakras flows. These channels are called meridians in Traditional Chinese Medicine (TCM). The Nadis, or meridians, direct the activity of the physical channels through which energy flows, including the nerves, bones, joints, muscles, ligaments, and glands. Marma and acupuncture points are points on the human body beneath which these vital channels intersect. The application of marma therapy or acupuncture can fix disruption in the flow of vital energy.

Air or breath and food form the nutritive QI. Nutritive QI travels through the meridians to all the tissues in the body. According to TCM, we inherit the third source of QI from your parents. We can call it the genetic energy force. The Chinese refer to it as original QI. Ayurveda also states that foods and breath, or air, contain prana or life energy.

This chapter will mainly consider the air aspect of prana or Qi and how we can revitalize the chakras through proper breathing. I have been practicing these breathing exercises for quite some time, and they help keep my energy levels up. While doing these exercises, it is essential to have the proper mindset because our intention and attention make the exercise effective.

Intention and attention

Every feeling has an emotion attached to it, which we express as happiness, anger, Joy, or sadness. Negative feelings, which are subtle thoughts, deplete our energy and cause the energy in the chakras to slow its flow. Positive feelings increase the energy flow. One way to increase the energy flow in the chakras is by putting our attention on the specific chakra and having the intention of increasing or revitalizing it. Energy flows where attention goes. Intention gives a direction to the energy and attention causes the energy to flow in that direction. The more we hold our attention to a particular point or area in the body, the more we enliven the area.

Breathing and the chakras

Air is the most vital substance for sustaining life. Air is energy in motion. Without a few minutes of air, we will succumb. When we breathe, we take in the energy from the air, which is called prana or life force. When we breathe in and out, having the intention and putting our attention on the chakras, we allow the prana to revitalize and nourish the chakras, assisting them in increasing their energy flow. The energy in the chakras moves in a spiral. If we move our body in a circular motion when we breathe in and out, we will facilitate the flow of energy in the chakras. Ancient rituals such as the dervish dance from the middle east, the American Indians, and in many cultures do circular movements in their spiritual rituals to heighten spiritual experiences. Similarly, Tai Chi and Qi Gong also incorporate circular movement with the breath to increase the life force.

Breathing Exercises

There are specific breathing exercises that can enhance the energy in various parts of the body. Here are a few you can practice.

Taking abdominal breaths is the natural and right way to breathe, whether you are standing, sitting, or walking. When taking in a long breath, the abdominal expands first, then the lungs or chest. Always breathe in and out through the nose and not the mouth and start by first exhaling.

Exercise 1: The Breath of Life

Do this exercise three times a day before starting the other exercises.

Take a full, long, deep breath. Start by breathing out first and squeezing the air out of the abdomen by tightening the stomach muscles as when you say Ha!. Breathe in by first filling the stomach until the abdomen is fully extended. Continue breathing in as you fill the chest cavity. Hold the breath for three-five seconds, then slowly breathe out, gradually drawing the abdomen in and up. When the air is forced out of the lungs by contracting the abdomen, take another breath, and continue to breathe this way, all the time holding the chest up, so there is very little motion in it.

Do not strain. The breathing should be deep but smooth and easy. While doing this exercise with the eyes closed, focus on the entire body, feeling the flow of energy pouring throughout the body, nourishing the whole physiology with vital life energy.

Exercise 2: Increasing circulation to the brain cells, nourishing the seventh and sixth Chakras.

Stand erect, heels together, the toes at an angle of thirty or thirty-five degrees. Extend the arms, right and left, to their utmost, so they are level with the shoulders. Palms facing upward, body from the waist thrown sightly forward. Clasp the hands tightly so that the muscles are rigid while tensing the muscles of the entire body. Now lift the hands slowly upwards until they meet over the head. Relax the muscles and return to the former position.

Inhale as you bring the hands up and exhale as you bring the hands down. Keep the attention on the head, having the intention to purify and nourish the brain cells and increase the flow of energy throughout the brain. Repeat about five to eight times. All the exercises follow the breathing pattern as described in the first exercise.

Exercise 3: Increasing circulation in the neck and throat, nourishing the fifth Chakra.

Stand as in exercise 2; arms extended, hands facing forward. Tense all the muscles, breathe in slowly as you slowly bring the arms to the front until the hands meet in front. Now bring the hands toward the chest by bending the elbows while maintaining the tension in the muscles. Hold for about three-five secs, then slowly release all the tension as you turn the palms to face outwards and move the palms of the hand in a pushing motion away from the body, breathing out slowly. With the hands fully extended, bring the hands back to the starting position. Relax. Repeat three-five times. Have the attention on the fifth and fourth chakras, having the intention of removing all the impurities from these areas, increasing circulation and vital energy to nourish every cell in these areas of the body.

Exercise 4: Increasing circulation in the chest and abdomen, nourishing the fourth and third chakras and marma points around the abdomen.

Stand with feet wide apart and hands extended level with the shoulder, palms facing upwards. Take a deep breath in as you bend backward from the waist, head tilted backward. Now bend forward, keeping the knees and legs straight as you breathe out, bringing the hands forward and downwards between the legs. Hold the position for three secs. Start breathing in as you slowly straighten the body, returning to the original position with the body and head tilted backward. Repeat this five to eight times. Have the attention on the abdomen and chest areas with the intention to purify these areas and nourish the lungs, heart, liver, and stomach.

Exercise 5: Increasing circulation and energy in the kidneys and loin area, nourishing the second Chakra.

Stand as in exercise 2 with arms hanging down, hands open. The legs must be tensed, and the knees not allowed to bend through the whole exercise. Bring the arms forward, extend them at full length over the head, and then bend forward to touch your toes with the hands. Hold for three secs. Return to the starting position and repeat three to five times. Inhale as you raise the hands above the head and exhale as you bend forward to touch the feet. Have the attention on the kidneys and loins areas and the second chakra, which is midway between the navel and the pubic bone, with the intention of releasing all the negative and trapped energies in the areas, increasing circulation and vital energy in the areas.

Exercise 6: Hold it close

Lie on the floor with legs extended and hands by your side. Bend the knees and draw the legs up towards the body, keeping the feet on the floor. Now breathe in deeply as you raise the pelvic off the floor, tilting the pelvic upwards and tightening the muscles in that region. Hold it for three to five secs. Slowly lower the pelvic to the floor as you breathe out. Relax. Repeat three to five times. Have the attention on the second chakra with the intention to release the trapped energies and create increased circulation and nourishment to the pelvic, lower back hips, and loins.

Exercise 7: Increasing circulation and energy in the loins, hips, and 2nd chakra

Stand with feet facing forward, shoulder width apart, hands on the hips, knees slightly bent. Breathe in as you tilt the pelvic backward while keeping the rest of the body upright. Breathe out as you tilt the pelvic forwards and up. Hold for three secs. Breathe in as you tilt the pelvic backward. Repeat three to five times. Have the attention on the second chakra, hip, and loins with the intention of releasing the block energies, increasing circulation and nourishing the pelvic and groin areas, and removing the blocks in the second chakra.

Exercise 8. Releasing negative energy and increasing circulation and nourishing energy in the first chakra.

Stand with feet wide apart and toes pointing slightly outwards. Place hands on the hips. Now bend your knees as deep as you can. At the lowest point, rock the pelvic back and forth, tilting the pelvic as high as you can. Do this three times before returning to a straight position as you breathe in. Repeat at least three times. Have the attention on the root or the first chakra with the intention to release the negative energies and blocks in the area and increase the flow of vitalizing energy.

Exercise 9: Nourishing the entire body and enlivening all the chakras.

Stand with feet slightly apart. Bring your hands to the front of the body with palms together, facing upwards. Breathe in slowly by filling the abdominal cavity first. At the same time, you tighten the muscles in the hands and legs as you slowly raise the palms of your hand over the front of your body, moving slowly from the loins to the stomach, then chest, neck, face, and head, until the hands pass the top of the head. Then push the hands upwards towards the ceiling, keeping the tension and tightening all the muscles in the body. Hold for three to five secs. Release all the tension in the body as you slowly breathe out and lower the hands with the palms facing downwards, pushing in a downward direction down the center line of the body until the hands reach the groin area. Relax.

Repeat at least three to five times. When breathing in, have the intention to carry all the energies of the body from the root chakra through all the chakras to the top of the head. When breathing out, have the intention of bathing the various chakras with universal energy. Keep the attention on the various chakras as the hands reach each area.

A friend of mine, who was having some discomfort in the pelvic area while walking started doing the breathing exercises. He reported that after a few days, the discomfort disappeared.

Alternate Breathing

Another breathing exercise that can be practiced before meditation is alternate breathing. While sitting upright, cover the right nostril with the thumb and breathe out through the left nostril. Now breathe in through the left nostril. Cover the left nostril with the third and fourth fingers and breathe out through the right nostril. Breathe in through the right nostril and repeat the exercise for about three to five minutes with eyes closed. This helps to calm the mind and is good preparation for meditation.

Yoga Asanas

Another very useful way to revitalize the chakras is by doing yoga asanas. As in the breathing exercises, when doing the asanas (yoga postures), it is essential to have the attention focused. It would be best if you did Asanas slowly and should not force to reach any position. Stretch as far as is comfortable, then hold the position for a few seconds, as you keep the attention on the point of stretch. Various asanas help to open up different energy centers in the body. If you haven't done asanas before, I suggest you learn from a qualified instructor as it s crucial to breathe correctly and not strain during these exercises. I have been doing yoga asanas regularly since I was in my twenties. They help increase flexibility, strength, release tension, and nourish the organs and cells of the body.

CHAPTER 8

Beings of Light

An electromagnetic field, known as the aura, surrounds the human body. Clairvoyants see the aura as light energy fields surrounding the human form.

We are essentially Beings of light. The source from which our life springs is the same source that creates everything in the universe. Light fractures into colors. Colors have specific frequencies or sounds, and sound slowing in vibration creates form. In chapter one, we saw that Modern Quantum Field Theory calls this underlying field of energy and intelligence pervading the universe, The Unified Field. Ancient masters or seers called it the field of pure consciousness because during their meditations, as the mind experienced the subtlest state of the thinking process or thought, it transcends-goes beyond-thought and experiences consciousness in its pure form.

Scientific evidence of the existence of our light body

For centuries, artists have been drawing light around the images of holy men and women. In the 1900s, Dr. George de la Warr and Dr. Ruth Brown (De La Warr, 1966) created instruments to detect radiation from living tissues. They developed Radionics, a system of detection, diagnosis, and healing from a distance using the human biological energy field. Using pictures taken of the energy field of their patients, they were able to show the formations of diseases in living tissue, such as tumors and cysts within the liver, tuberculosis of the lungs, and malignant brain tumors.

In 1977 Franz Morell and his son-in-law, engineer Erich Rasche (in Germany), (Tansely, 1972) invented Bioresonance Therapy. These therapies use an energy field, whether electrical, magnetic, sonic, acoustic, microwave, infrared, or other, to screen for or treat health conditions by detecting imbalances in the body's energy field then attempting to correct them. Practitioners of energy medicine believe that imbalances in the body occur first in the bioenergetic fields. then in the chemical and structural areas of the body. Today we have bioenergetic medicine and instruments that can measure the imbalances and treat health conditions existing in the body energy fields.

Auras and light bodies

Researchers describe the human energy field as a luminous body that surrounds and interpenetrates the physical body. We usually call the radiation from this field the aura. Observations and experiments show that the Human Energy Field (HEF) has seven layers, sometimes called bodies, that interpenetrate and surround each other in successive layers.[7]

The aura extends beyond the physical body and acts as an external sensory mechanism connecting us with the surrounding environment. For instance, we can sense when someone enters our energy sphere. That is why we sometimes feel uncomfortable if someone is too close to us, and we can also feel someone looking at us even when we are not facing or seeing them. The light from their eyes touches our energy field, and we can sense the change. We sometimes say, the vibes are not good when we sense something is not right in our environment.

The various energy fields of our body are interconnected and affect our health, well-being, and spiritual growth. The more we can harmonize the energies between these different layers of ourselves, the more expanded our awareness and consciousness will be and the greater our health.

The seven layers of the aura are the physical, emotional, mental, astral, etheric, celestial, and ketheric. Further away from the physical body, the light body is the higher its vibration. The seven layers of the aura or light bodies are associated with the chakras. The first layer, which is nearest to the physical body, corresponds with the first chakra, and the second layer with the second chakra, and so on, each layer extending further away from the body. Also, the colors associated with each chakra correspond with the color associated with the light body.

---

[7] Hands of Light, Barbara Ann Brennan, Chapter 7, 1987, Bantam Books.

Chakras produce energy vortices, which, when healthy, provide the energetic information by which all the body systems create a global information system.[8] These findings correspond to similar discoveries made by Barbara Ann Brennan and Rosalyn Bruyere, both authors, healers, and clairvoyants, and have written extensively about chakras and auras.

I have studied light therapy and marma therapy and have used these systems to remove blockages in the chakras and energy centers in the body. Following is a brief description of both systems.

Maharishi Light Therapy with Gems (MLG)

A client of mine who suffered from hand and shoulder pains for several years because of his profession as a tile layer found great relief from the aches and discomforts with just a few treatments of Maharishi Light Therapy with Gems (MLG). During his treatment, I placed special light beamers containing precious stones, like a diamond, ruby, sapphires, etc., at varying heights above the chakras of his body. The light from the precious metals would shine on the chakras, enlivening the energy. As stated previously, each chakra controls various body functions. When the energy in the chakra is enhanced, healing takes place in the body.

The effect of light on human physiology is well known. For example, in winter, people suffer from depression caused by a lack of sunlight (SAD). Throughout the ages, in many traditional medicines, the warming energy of the sunlight and the cooling energy of moonlight have been used to heal the body.

MLG uses special gem beamers or light projectors that enhance the orderliness and nourishing qualities of precious stones.

---

[8] https://journals.sagepub.com/doi/10.1177/2164956119831221

When suitable light shines through gemstones, such as Diamonds, Emerald, Rubies, Blue Sapphires, and Yellow Sapphires, their molecular characteristics and healing properties get imprinted in the specific frequencies (spectrum) of the transmitted light. It then transferred to the body revitalizing the body's innate intelligence and restoring balance and health to the physiology.

MLG gently nourishes the finer aspects of physiological functioning associated with the body s nerve centers.

The specific molecular composition and orderly crystalline structure of these gemstones endow them with balancing and healing effects. The vibrations and information carried out by the light awaken and resonate with the body s own natural internal healing power.

This stimulates self-healing, cleanses and harmonizes the subtle levels of the body in a very pleasant and gentle way. The treatments are non-invasive, deeply relaxing, and enjoyable, and can produce blissful experiences.[9]

Maharishi Light Therapy with gems restores balance to the physical body and influences all the other light bodies that make up the individual energy field. Using light therapy is now a part of treatment in many hospitals throughout the world.

Marma and aroma Therapy

Marmas are vital points and energy fields that are essential for health, happiness, and long life in spiritual fulfillment. It is essential to remove the blocks in the chakras, and the techniques of breathing, light, aroma, and marma can all help to accomplish this.

---

[9] http://www.gem-light-therapy.com/

A few years ago, I attended a training course on Marma Therapy given by Dr. Ernst Schrott in Holland. Dr. Schrott is the author of Marma Therapy: The Healing Power of Ayurvedic Vital

Point Massage. He has studied for many years, under various masters of marma therapy, throughout India. He operates at the time of writing treatment centers in Germany, where he has been successfully treating patients for various ailments.

Dr. Schrott developed a very gentle technique for treating Marmas that brings inner tranquility and therefore has its primary effect on the level of consciousness and then on the body and its organs. It is called Sukshma, or gentle Marma treatment. In Sukshma Marma

Therapy, the primary attention is on the energetic aspects of the Marma points: the field of consciousness of the Marmas. (Schrott, 2016).

Marmas are subtle, intelligent, and powerful control points in the mind and body. The marma points on the surface of the body contain information about the physiology, physical organs and systems, and the state of our emotions and consciousness. They also let us see and sense the auras around individuals. Marmas, especially the main marmas of the chakras, are the powerhouses of the body and act as junction points between mind, body, and consciousness. They are the connections between the physical body, the various light bodies, and the cosmos.

In Sukshma Marma Therapy, the treatment involves healing with the hands. Our hands have great healing powers. Our hands are full of Marmas, large and small, and these give us the sensitivity to feel mentally and physically, informing the way we move our hands and the way we touch. The fingers and palms of the hand have subtle energy-prana-flowing out of them.

During treatment, as we touch the various marma points on the body, we send healing energy from our hands into the marmas with our attention on these points. Unlike regular massage, in Sukshma Marma

Therapy, the touch is very gentle, with the therapist pausing in silence during every touch. It is in the silence that transformation takes place.

Aroma Therapy

During marma treatments, special organic herbal essential oils are used to treat various conditions. For thousands of years, essential oils have been used to soothe and heal the body. We all have our favorite scents, such as rose, lavender, or citrus, that make us feel relaxed or energized. In marma therapy, we apply the oils directly to the skin at the marma points. The oils penetrate the skin and aid in stimulating the marma and the surrounding tissues and cells.

Choosing the correct oils for marma therapy is very important because part of the healing effects come from the plant ingredients and the aromatic substance the marma receives. For Vata disorders, sweet almond, sesame, and jojoba oils are suitable. For Pitta disorders, you can use coconut, sunflower oil, or ghee. For Kapha disorders, use oils that stimulate the metabolism, such as rosemary, pine, ginger, clove, and camphor oil.

We can treat the marmas through any of the five senses, touch, sound, sight, smell, and taste. Also, because we are dealing with energy fields, we can also treat the marmas without actually touching the body. The hands placed above the body can transmit energy or prana into the marma and is as effective as touching. The more developed the consciousness of the therapist, the greater the effect will be.

When we view the body as energy fields, we can understand the relationship between chemicals, foods, light, sound, and their effects on the body. Whatever we take in through our five senses is essentially a form of energy. It can either enhance our well-being or decrease our well-being. This brings us to the final sheath of the body, the grossest physical level, Annamaya Kosha: The outer sheath is the body layer muscles, bones, skin, organs.

CHAPTER 9

Annamayakosha– The outer body sheath

A nna means food, which is what sustains this level of the physical system. Food is not just what we eat. Anything that we take in through the five senses can be food. The air we breathe, the scents we smell, the things we hear, what we touch and feel all impact the energies in our body. Sound, light, and touch are ways we transmit energy from one person or thing to another. And we have seen in the previous chapters that thought is also energy. The thoughts we have about ourselves and others can either nourish or deplete our energy. In fact, the most important foods you eat every day are your thoughts.

Our thoughts are very powerful energy fields, arising from an infinite energy field within our self. Therefore, they affect every aspect of our physiology. We know that if we continue to have negative thoughts and feelings, we can feel tired, and it can lead to depression, indigestion, insomnia, and a host of other ailments. A negative feeling can make us lose our appetite.

In chapter four and chapter five, we saw how our emotions and thinking affect our spiritual and material life. I advise you to review these chapters and complete the exercises to help you master your emotions. To decrease negative thoughts, look at your values and beliefs that are causing you to have certain emotions.

107

We are constantly interacting with our environment through our senses. Wherever our attention goes, energy flows. Whatever we expose ourselves to during the day also affects the state of our health- the air we breathe, the things we see and hear, taste, and touch. Some individuals can drain our energy; others can make us feel uplifted.

Associate with people who inspire and uplift you, and keeping your attention on uplifting and inspiring things will enhance your level of happiness. As much as possible, avoid negative people and conversations as they will drain you.

Food energetics

We convert the foods we eat into energy within the body. Food acts as the fuel that makes our body function. The quality of the food, method of preparation, and the emotional and mental state of the cook, all play an essential part in how nourishing the food will be for our body. Have you ever eating from someone who has been in a foul mood? I am sure that the food did not feel very satisfying. One reason prayer is said before meals in many traditions is to remove the negative influences that the food may have received from the influence of the cook and others. Through prayers, we put our attention and infuse positive energy into the meal.

Ayurveda and Traditional Chinese Medicine (TCM) emphasize the type of energy in different foods. They base the suitability of food for an individual on his constitution or body type. According to TCM, some people are more Yin (cold), others more Yang (hot) or a combination of Yin and Yang. Similarly, in Ayurveda, individuals can be Vata, Pitta, or Kapha, or a combination of these three elements. Ayurveda also defines foods in this manner. Some foods are more heated, others more cooling, and others have a neutral effect on the body. Knowing your body type and what foods suit you is very helpful to maintain good health. Let's take a closer look at the different body types in Ayurveda.

The Doshas

Doshas are the three vital energies in Ayurveda and comprise the five elements (fire, water, earth, ether, and air). Every Dosha comprises two of those five elements, with one dominating and one subordinate element. Ayurveda views these Doshas as the dynamic forces responsible for all the processes within our body and mind. They describe physical characteristics and mental preferences. Ayurveda aims to keep the Doshas in balance as an overly powerful influence of one Dosha can cause all kinds of undesirable conditions. Their names Vata, Pitta, and Kapha are Sanskrit terms used to describe the Doshas. Listed below is a description of each Dosha.

Vata: Air, Ether the movement principle. Light, cold, dry, mobile, subtle, and rough.

Pitta: Fire, Water the energy principle. Light, hot, greasy, sharp, and fluid.

Kapha: Water, Earth the structure principle. Heavy, cold, greasy, stable, and softening.

To easily understand the Doshas, think of a car: it has wheels, giving the car its mobility; this is Vata. It has an internal combustion engine that creates the energy to move the car; this is Pitta. It has a chassis that provides the overall structure of the car; this is Kapha.

Most people are dominated by one or two of the Doshas, and they come into the picture in different and individual ways. All Doshas always exist side by side, their relation to each other constantly changing. In fact, they are not different energies, but just different sides of one energy. Every two Doshas share one characteristic, whereas the third one is the opposite. It is through this principle of opposites that keep the Doshas in balance.

In trying to understand the Doshas, try to feel their influences. For example, a windy day would add Vata energy to the overall balance because it has a cooling and drying influence.

To keep your Doshas balanced, you first have to find out which Dosha or combination of them is dominant in your body. Preferably, an experienced practitioner of Ayurveda will assist you in determining this. Once you observe yourself, it will get easier to see the influences that steer your actions, thoughts, and feelings. Understanding them (and thus yourself) better helps immensely to stay in control and keep your life in balance.

The Six Tastes in Ayurveda

Taste plays an essential part in the foods we eat. Following is a list of the six tastes and the elements associated with them. The combination of these factors can affect a wide range of responses in different individuals. While each substance is certainly unique, each of the six tastes exerts a somewhat predictable influence on our physiology.

The 6 Tastes and Their Predominant Elements

Sweet " Earth & Water: Derived from water and earth element influences. It increases Kapha and reduces Vata and Pitta. Examples of foods with a sweet taste are grains and complex carbohydrates, milk, butter, and cashews. Sweet taste is best obtained from complex carbohydrates and sweeteners (in moderation) so that their post-digestive effects result from digestion. The sweet taste of ordinary foods nourishes and builds the body. Many of the foods recommended for rejuvenation are sweet when well-masticated and have a sweet post-digestive effect.

Sour " Earth & Fire: Derived from fire and earth elements. It increases pitta and Kapha and decreases Vata. Some foods with a sour taste are citrus and some other fruits, hard cheeses, and yogurt, which is needed in small quantities.

Salty "Water & Fire: Derived from fire and water element influences. It increases pitta and Kapha and decreases Salt helps in maintaining mineral balance and retaining water. It can usually be found in foods.

Pungent " Fire & Air: Derived from air and fire element influences. Increases Vata and pitta and reduces Kapha. It is in hot peppers, ginger, cumin, and some other spices. It is needed for metabolism, stimulates appetite and digestion.

Bitter " Air & Ether: Derived from ether and air element influences. It increases Vata and decreases pitta and Kapha. It is found in spinach and some other green leafy vegetables, eggplant, and turmeric. It helps detoxify the body, hence its use in some medicinal preparations for cleansing the body.

Astringent " Air & Earth: Derived from ether and earth element influences. It increases Vata and decreases pitta and Kapha. It is found in beans, lentils, and some fruits and helps maintain the firmness of the tissues.

Ayurveda: Attributes of Certain Foods

Every food item contains some twenty properties proportion of the Five basic elements (Space, Air, Fire, Water & Earth), with one or more dominant elements. The three Doshas and seven tissue systems also have different proportions of the five basic elements, with a dominance of certain elements in each.

According to the Ayurvedic principle of like increases & dislike decreases, foods having the properties of a particular dosha and/ or tissue systems increase those properties. When foods have opposite properties, it results in a decrease in those properties. These properties (or Gunas in Sanskrit) are 20 in number and are distributed amongst the five basic elements.

Ayurveda evaluates our diet based on the tastes and its effect on the Doshas and the following energetic qualities of the food: Temperature: cold or warm; Weight: light or heavy; and Moisture: dry or wet.

The Ayurvedic approach treats what you are like right now, and takes it one day, one season at a time. When you wish to bring balance into your digestion, look at what qualities and tastes dominate in your diet and balance them with the opposite qualities.

These twenty properties are classified in opposing pairs of tens and are listed as:

Heavy Light
Cold Hot
Unctuous Dry
Slow Sharp
Stable Mobile
Soft Hard Slimy
Rough
Viscous Liquid
Gross Subtle
Cloudy Clear

Here are some examples of how the 20 properties exhibit themselves in various Foods:

Heavy Cream, Cheese, Kidney Beans.
Light Puffed Rice, Popcorn.
Cold Mint, Coconut Water, Watermelon, Rice.
Hot Peppers, Nutmeg, Turkey Meat.
Qily Nuts, Fats, And Qils, Black Lentil.

Dry Millet, Rye, Corn.

Slow Yogurt, Red Meat, Condensed Milk.

Sharp Onion, Ginger, Garlic, Bell Peppers, Mustard Greens.

Stable Ghee, Wheat.

Mobile Alcohol, Sprouts.

Soft Puffed Rice, Tapioca, Pasta.

Hard Nuts, Jack Fruit.

Slimy Okra, Full Cream Yogurt.

Rough Most Millets, Broccoli, Cauliflower, Oats.

Dense Cream, Potatoes.

Liquid All Water-Based Beverages, Soups, Milk.

Gross Roots And Tubers, Dates, Minerals.

Subtle Spices, Saffron, Oils

Cloudy Mayonnaise, Butter, Sea Food.

Clear Clarified Butter Milk, Black-Eyed Pea, Bitters.

Basic Dietary Rules That Ayurveda Recommends

Following are some basic dietary rules that are recommended to maintain a healthy lifestyle.

1. Eat Food That Nourishes: Eating fresh is the best. We get the maximum nutrients from seasonal locally grown foods. Our bodies are made to process natural whole foods rather than processed foods. Choose whole grains over refined ones, whole fruits, and lots of seasonal vegetables. Go organic for the maximum benefits.

2. Balanced Diet: A simple formula for this- include the six Ayurvedic tastes or Rasas: sweet, sour, salty, bitter, pungent, and astringent in every meal. Ayurveda states that including all six tastes in every meal will ensure a balanced meal and a

feeling of satisfaction, preventing snacking and overeating. It also makes the meal look more attractive and appealing.

3. Load Up on Fruits and Vegetables: Color your plate deep blue, purple, red, green, or orange. These are the richest sources of antioxidants and nutrients that help boost immunity. So, load up on fruits and vegetables, as they are great internal cleansers too.

4. Make Nutrition Bioavailable: When we eat raw vegetables, the digestive system takes time to work through the layers to reach the core and release nutrients eating them cooked means more efficient digestion. Ayurveda recommends that eating sauteed, steamed, and cooked vegetables help the digestive process. If you want to eat salads, then lunch is the time to do so.

5. Spice Up: Spices are an integral part of our daily meals. They add to the taste, but very few realize spices add to a meals' nutritional value too. They enhance digestion, promoting the absorption of nutrients to the maximum. Spices also add to the Ayurvedic principle of including all the rasas (tastes) in a meal.

6. Cleanse Out: Ayurveda staunchly believes that when our digestive energy- Agni is robust, we are in a state of balance and health. However, if our digestion is not good, we build up Ama- an accumulation of digestive toxins. To avoid this, we must eat away from our computer or TV, in a peaceful atmosphere.

Eat when you are actually hungry; let the body set the time. Eat at a moderate pace, neither gulping nor too slowly.

Ayurveda also recommends a complete cleanse in every change of season, especially at the start of spring. It is also good to go on a liquid fast one day in the week. This will allow the body to clear out toxins. You can have fruit or vegetable juices during the day, but it should not be cold. Also, drinking hot water during the day you are fasting will assist in the process.

7. Drink Water: The key is to keep yourself hydrated and energized with water, preferably warm to flush out the toxin. Ice cold water is a bad idea; cool or room temperature is healthy. Caffeine, aerated sodas, and alcohols are not really vitality-boosting drinks! Go easy.

Ayurvedic Tips For Healthy Digestion

People are constantly on the go, and most do not take the proper time to eat. Many eat while reading, watching TV, or at business meetings. Eating is one of the most important activities that we do daily. No wonder why many people suffer from occasional digestion problems: gas, bloating, stomach discomfort, constipation, heartburn, and fatigue after eating.

For optimal digestion, our bodies need a suitable environment for digestion to start: an uplifting and settled environment allows the body to process and absorb the nutrients from our meals. If that isn't available, Ayurvedic experts advise at least be sitting down to eat. Standing, walking, driving, and other similar activities can inhibit digestion. When we sit down to eat, and our stomach is relaxed, our awareness is on the taste, texture, and smell of the food, it will enhance digestion.

Balancing your digestive fire Agni is a key principle. That's why Ayurveda recommends several general practices for better digestion. We can compare digestive Agni to a burning fire. If the flame is very low, it will take a long time to cook the food. In the same way, if the fire is too big, it can burn the food. If we put a huge log on a low fire, it will extinguish it. The goal is to balance our digestive fires so we digest our meals efficiently and smoothly.

Another way to improve digestion is to stimulate the Agni, or digestive fire, before we eat. Weak digestive Agni may cause fatigue after eating. To handle this, eat a teaspoon of grated fresh ginger with a few drops of lemon juice and a few pinches of salt on it before a full meal. This blend of spices activates the salivary glands, producing the enzymes necessary to help digest the nutrients in the food and help support absorption by the body.

The ginger-and-lemon juice recommendation helps to increase the digestive power. If, however, you suffer from an overactive Agni, because of which there is too much internal heat and acid, then Pomegranate Chutney may be more suitable for you.

Ayurveda and Traditional Chinese Medicine (TCM) recommend avoiding cold drinks at meals and ice-cold foods. This is because it weakens Agni it's like putting cold water on the burning logs. Iced water, usually served at restaurants, extinguishes the digestive fire. Even juice or milk right out of the refrigerator is too cold for digestion. We should take juice at room temperature and water without ice. Once you get into this habit of drinking beverages at room temperature, you will notice a dramatic improvement in your digestion and how your body feels while eating and after the meal. Cold drinks and foods mixed with warm cooked foods can cause stomach cramps, bloating, and general discomfort in the stomach area.

If you have a Pitta imbalance, you can take cool drinks in between meals. We do not recommend cold or frozen foods for Pitta because, even though they may temporarily cool down the heat, the Agni is still being overstimulated. The imbalance will continue. Try slightly cool drinks made with Organic Rose Water or milk blended with dates or fresh mangoes.

The next recommendation has to do with the time of the day that you eat your meals. Have you ever gone out for a late dinner and found that it was a strain to wake up the following day or that it was challenging to be efficient during the next day? These are often the side effects of improperly digested food. The best way to avoid these problems is to follow nature's prescription for suitable times to eat. Digestive strength is closely tied to the solar cycle. When the sun is strongest between 12 and 2 p.m. is when the digestive fire is also strong. Ayurveda associates Agni with the sun.

Dinner should be lighter than lunch and should ideally eat dinner before 8:00 p.m. Late-night meals interfere with sleep, and after 10:00 p.m., the body is working to burn off toxins and continues to digest food from the day. If you eat after 10:00 p.m., the food may cause toxins to accumulate in the system, and as a result, you wake up tired the next day. If you cannot wake up fresh and alert, then it's important to analyze the quantity of food and the time of night you are eating dinner.

Another Ayurvedic tip for digestion is to drink a fresh yogurt drink called lassi at lunchtime. Sweet lassi consists of 1/4 cup fresh homemade yogurt, 1 cup room-temperature water, and sugar to taste. Blend it for one minute in the blender. Lassi is light and contains lactobacilli, necessary bacteria that lubricate the intestines to help digestion go smoothly. Lassi drinks help to reduce gas and bloating. They also taste delicious and can make a meal more satisfying and nutritious.

Good nutrition goes beyond eating foods that are fresh and wholesome. If the digestion process is sluggish, your body creates sticky food residue called ama that can clog the channels in the body and hinder the process of assimilation. Proper digestion and metabolism result in the conversion of the foods you eat into healthy body tissues.

Here are some basic Ayurveda routines that you can try.

The regimen of Personal Daily routine (Dinacharya)

Wake up early, at least one hour before sunrise. Attending nature's call - bowels, urination, etc. Never suppress nor forcefully void the natural urges - suppression can lead to many diseases.

Liver flush- Have a hot glass of water with a few drops of lemon or lime juice first thing in the morning to flush out the toxins released by the liver during the night.

Breathe- Do the breathing exercises as described in the seventh chapter. Do at least the life-breath if you are short on time. This will revitalize the energies in the body.

Yoga Asana- To prepare the body for meditation. Meditate- At least twenty minutes in the morning and evening.

Nasal drops (Nasya)- Put two drops of sesame oil/ mustard oil/ ghee or Anu Tali (An Ayurvedic medicine if available)- It is supposed to prevent premature greying of hair baldness and ensures good sleep.

Mouth wash - Fill mouth with Triphala (Ayurvedic medicine) decoction or other medicated oils - It prevents excess thirst, improves taste, and maintains oral hygiene. It is also useful in managing the mouth ulcers and dryness commonly seen in Diabetes patients.

Oleation (Abhyanga) "applying a variety of oils, such as Sesame oil, on a daily basis" keeps the skin soft, improves blood circulation, and removes waste. This helps in the prevention of numbness of extremities. Applying Sesame oil or any suitable oil on the head in sufficient quantity, which enhances the strength of the head and forehead and makes hair black, long, and deep-rooted.

Exercise - Exercising early in the morning can help remove stagnation in the body and can help recharge and rejuvenate your body and mind for a productive day. Regular exercise is an important step for the prevention and management of various ailments.

Bath - Taking a bath half to one hour after exercise - Prevents premature greying of hair, baldness, ensures good sleep and physical hygiene.

Food -we should follow the various aspects as mentioned in the topic on diet. Although foods are supposed to provide us with proper nutrition, most foods are lacking in nutritional value. To increase your nutritional intake, I recommend you include a good probiotic, as well as multivitamins and collagen supplements in your diet.

Sleep - Keep the environment clean and pleasant. Avoid sleeping during the day. Proper sleep provides health and longevity. Improves complexion and glow.

One should take proper sleep every night, which should be between 6-8 hours per night. In summer, one can take a small nap during the daytime as well. Too much sleep and too little sleep both are not good for healthy living. Sleeping in the day is not advisable.

Ayurvedic Behavioral Rasayanas (rejuvenation)

Our attitude towards others plays an essential role in our health. Some basic principles on behavior are prescribed in Ayurveda, called behavioral rasayanas, that enhance health, happiness, and longevity. These behavioral rasayanas improve our ability to make positive behavioral choices, assisting us in avoiding mistakes that can cause ill health and unhappiness. Here are a few of them.

Speak the sweet truth. Speak the truth, but say it in a way that is not harsh or rough. Avoid speaking when you are angry, as the truth may not likely be sweet. Try to find a pleasant way to convey a truthful message. When correcting, it is a good practice to say something first that is uplifting. This puts the person in a good frame of mind to listen, and they are less likely to take offense when you point out some mistake or what they may have done wrong. We should speak in a way that does not damage the feelings of the other. The feeling level is the most tender level of life. When we damage the feelings of another, it takes a long while for healing to take place. Speaking lies creates ama or impurities in our bodies.

Stay free of anger. Anger is like a fire that consumes all in its path. When you feel angry, take a couple of slow deep breaths to calm yourself.

Harboring anger destroys your bliss, makes you unhappy, and affects your health. It is not worth it. One way of overcoming anger is to realize that your being angry is harming you. Perhaps you were wrongfully accused or were spoken to in an unkind manner. Keep in mind that everyone is their own responsibility. You are not responsible for how someone acts or thinks. You are responsible for how you act and think. If you did something wrong, then apologize and move on. People's behavior towards us is like a gift someone brings to you. You have a choice to accept or reject the gifts. If someone says some unkind words to you, you don t have to accept their negative gifts. Leave them with it. Don't keep thinking about what they said, as this will be like accepting their gifts, and it will poison you. Don't give up your bliss for the trash of the world.

You can also practice forgiveness. In practicing forgiveness, it's also important to forgive yourself, or that anger will reflect on others. Stress causes people to say and do the wrong things. This is why it is important to take care of your stress with meditation, exercises, and proper rest.

Be respectful to teachers and elders. Unfortunately, these days there is so much disrespect for elders, teachers, and even parents. Teachers and elders can teach us invaluable lessons by sharing their wisdom and experience. It's easy to read a book to gain knowledge, but it's often very difficult to apply it in daily life. An elder or teacher can tell you how they tried to practice unconditional forgiveness, for instance, and what the results were. Only wise elders can share such valuable life experiences.

They are the best guides. It is when one respects teachers and elders that they will offer their advice freely.

Practice meditation and stay balanced in sleep and wakefulness. By practicing the Transcendental Meditation technique twice, a day, you open your mind to pure consciousness, releasing stress and strengthening the intellect to allow you to make healthy choices in life. You'll find yourself naturally growing in positive behaviors without strain or effort.

Along with the practice of meditation, it's good to follow the ayurvedic routine of rising before 6:00 a.m. and sleeping before 10:00 at night. This allows your body and mind to become attuned with nature's rhythms, creating maximum clarity and alertness during the day and deep rest at night. It is when people are tired and stressed that many behavioral problems begin. All of the ayurvedic routines (massage, exercise, yoga, eating the main meal at noon and eating lightly at night) help promote positive behavior.

Eat pure foods. Eating pure organic foods suitable to your body will help you maintain good health and improve your mental and physical well-being. Impure foods, such as stale foods, leftovers, and processed foods, tend to have diminished life force (prana). It may taste good but will not be nourishing to the body. Keep in mind that food is anything we take in through the five senses, so pay attention to what you expose yourself to.

Keep the company of the wise. It is important to stay in the company of the wise, to choose like-minded friends who will support your desire to follow a pure spiritual path. We all have latent tendencies that are waiting for the opportunity to rise up. Hanging out with negative people and in negative environments will allow these tendencies to sprout.

CHAPTER 10

Exercise

Regular exercise is important to take care of our physical body. Remember, we are energy beings. When we move, we increase the flow of energy in our body. The health benefits associated with regular exercise are many. Specifically, exercise can help prevent heart disease and stroke, high blood pressure, obesity, back pain, osteoporosis. In addition, it can help fight depression and promote improved stress management.

To maximize your overall health benefits, I typically recommend you perform twenty to thirty minutes of aerobic activity three or more times a week and some muscle-strengthening activity and stretching at least twice a week. However, you can also achieve significant health benefits by completing thirty minutes or more of moderate- intensity physical activity a day, at least five times a week. Before starting any exercise program, especially if you have some existing health condition, be sure to check first with your healthcare provider or physician. When starting an exercise routine, take into consideration your age, fitness level, and health. If you haven t exercised for a while, start slowly. Don t run a mile on your first day.

Suppose you are just starting an exercise program. In that case, start at a slow pace with low-impact activities such as walking or swimming will allow you to improve your physical fitness level while safeguarding you from unwanted overuse injuries and burnout. Once you get in better shape, you can gradually integrate more strenuous and varied activities into your routine.

Positive Impact of Physical Activity

Regular physical activity reduces the risk of developing or dying from some leading causes of illness and death. Further, regular exercise effectively:

- It reduces the risk of dying from heart disease.
- It reduces the risk of developing diabetes.
- It reduces the risk of developing high blood pressure.
- It helps reduce blood pressure in people who already have high blood pressure.
- It reduces the risk of developing colon cancer.
- It reduces feelings of depression and anxiety.
- It helps control weight.
- It helps build and maintain healthy bones, muscles, and joints.
- It helps older adults become stronger and better able to move about without falling.
- It promotes psychological well-being.

Virtually everyone, regardless of age, sex, race, or physical ability, can achieve health benefits from exercise. Therefore, if you want to feel better, have more energy, and live longer, simply follow a regular, moderate exercise program and enjoy a better quality of life.

DAVID LEE SHENG TIN, HHC, PH.D

Five Simple Exercise Tips

Tip #1 Do Something You Enjoy

Exercise doesn't have to mean spending hours at the gym peddling away on a stationary bike. It doesn't mean you have to spend money on exercise gadgets you will probably never use, either. Anything you do to get your body moving is going to be better than doing nothing. Walking is a simple exercise that you can do just about anywhere, in any climate. Bike riding, dancing, gardening, weight lifting, swimming, playing a favorite sport, house cleaning, and even playing in the yard with your children are just a few ways you can add exercise into your daily routine. For strength, you can do push up, pull up, plank, and squats. Yoga and Pilates offer good stretching and strengthening exercises.

Tip #2 Schedule Time for Exercise

As you would a meeting or a doctor appointment, sometimes the only way to make time to exercise is to put it on your daily schedule. We ve all got busy lives, and we re often so busy taking care of others that we never seem to make time for ourselves. Once exercise becomes part of your daily To-Do list, you re more likely to do it. Some people set a specific time of the day to do their exercise, while others will have to vary each day. Some people need a nudge and for them, exercising with a friend is a wonderful solution. Choose whichever way works best for you. Just remember to actually do it!

Tip #3 Remember that Exercise Can Energize

Even though you might feel too tired to exercise, try it anyway. It might surprise you to find how energized you feel while you re at it and afterward when you re finished. Exercise is a great stress-reliever too, and if you know anything about stress, you know it is one of the body s biggest energy-sappers.

Tip #4 Don't Be Afraid to Mix it up

Like anything that is done repeatedly, exercise can become mundane. When you get bored with exercising, you re less likely to keep at it. To keep from getting bored with your workout routine, change it. If you re tired of walking, try cycling. If you re into weight lifting, try alternating this with cardiovascular exercises throughout the week. Go bowling or play a game of tennis once in a while, and if you find you enjoy these types of activities, join up with a team.

Tip #5 Always Begin by Warming up

Regardless of the type of exercise you choose, you need to begin each session by warming up your muscles. Stretching helps prevent damage to muscle tissue, and it gets your blood flowing. It gets your heart pumping, too. Just five minutes is all it takes to get your exercise session off to a good start.

There are many good exercise routines on the internet. You can choose those that appeal to you. The important thing is to be consistent if you want to see results. As we move the energies in our body, we will feel happier and healthier.

CHAPTER 11

A Vision of Possibilities

We are born to enjoy, to experience the fullness of life. Many people struggle to experience happiness daily and settle for a few moments of pleasure during the day that makes them feel good. As light Beings, emerging from a universal source of pure intelligence and energy, you are born with infinite potential. However, as we have seen, education, family, culture, and society, blind us from the reality of our nature. We forget the joy and innocence we knew as a child. The stress and strains, the programming that we undergo through education, religion, and society, rob us of the ability to experience the inner bliss of our true self. That state of bliss consciousness is always there within. When we turn our attention within and experience it, we remember how sweet we are. If you have reached this far in the book, you would have discovered that you are more than your mind and body.

In my years of teaching meditation, I recognize that most people are only aware of three states of consciousness; waking, dreaming, and sleep. From my own personal experience and that of many others around the world, who have been meditating (especially TM meditation), realize other states of consciousness, such as, Transcendental Consciousness, Cosmic Consciousness, Refined Cosmic Consciousness, sometimes referred to as God Consciousness, and Unity Consciousness. These higher states of consciousness are the birthright of every individual. They open the awareness to greater levels of happiness, freedom, creativity, and love.

The first state of awakening is the inner experience during meditation of transcendental consciousness. In that state, the mind and body experience deep rest, and the brain gains maximum coherence. The stresses dissolve from the mind and body. The daily activity becomes more enjoyable and fruitful. Here are some experiences of people having their first experience of bliss in meditation.

"After my second day of TM meditation, I was just floating in bliss. I started to smile without any reason. I left the TM center with a wide grin on my face. I felt extremely energetic. I decided to walk home instead of taking a taxi. The TM center at that time was near a huge open area in Port of Spain, Trinidad, known as the Savanah. I walked around this big park and just kept on feeling intense bliss inside. It seemed the colors of the flowers in the park were glowing, even moving, jumping out at me. The sky seemed bluer and brighter, everything seemed to appear millions of times more beautiful, and I realized that it was all because of the experience I had in my meditation. The meditation opened my reservoir of inner bliss that was hidden inside of me, enriching any outer experience I was having."
RR Brazil

"The first time I closed my eyes to meditate, I felt an upsurge of bliss that I never expected to have. I was seventeen years old and seeking to find a greater purpose in life outside of material wealth. Over the years, I continue to experience bliss and deep silence during meditation. This inner experience translates into a sense of being anchored in life to something higher than my small self. I always feel that no matter what challenges happen in my life, I have an inner sanctum of strength and calm to pull me through. I now know true inner wealth along with outer success in life." M B, NY USA

The second stage occurs when the nervous system is pure enough to allow the individual to maintain the inner experience of silence, fullness, and happiness in daily activity. This state is Cosmic Consciousness, also known as the state of self-realization or enlightenment. In this state, you live in harmony with all the laws of nature; you become a witness to all your activities, waking, dreaming, and sleeping. Here is an experience from a friend who had a glimpse of Cosmic Consciousness during sleep.

The sages consider Cosmic Consciousness normal state of life that you are born to live. This is the state of life, free from suffering, worries, and anxieties. This natural state has always been available to us, as it is our very nature. However, our constant outward focus overshadows our inner state, and we forget the beauty, peace, and love that exist within us.

Usually, when we look at an object, such as a flower, we lose awareness of our inner bliss as the object captures our attention. With the attention focused outward, we lose the connection to our divine self. Losing the ability to experience happiness and love continuously, we chase after love and happiness in faces and places. Since everyone is seeking the same thing, there is competition among us to get the best and hold on to what we have at all costs. When we feel unhappy, unloved, we blame others or feel bad about ourselves, sometimes wondering, what is wrong with me?

We teach our children that if they do not get a proper education and work hard, they will never be happy. Having worked with many successful people over the years, I have seen how untrue this is. So many successful people are unhappy, unhealthy, and unfulfilled, despite all the money they have accumulated. I have also met individuals from all around the world who live a very simple life, and they are much happier and more loving than their successful counterparts. I am not suggesting that material success is not important. On the contrary, it is important to live two hundred percent of your life, one hundred percent outer achievement, and one hundred percent inner development. We should not sacrifice one for the other unless we chose to be a monk or recluse.

The next stage of development is Refined Cosmic Consciousness (Refined CC). In this state, your perception of the environment becomes more refined. Objects appear as energy particles of light, and you experience a deeper connection between you and the object/s of perception. Not that the object, for instance, a chair, is no longer seen as a chair, but while you perceive the chair as a solid object, you also see the vibrating fields of light that make up the chair. The world seems brighter and filled with light. Because you already establish the state of pure consciousness on the level of the conscious mind in Cosmic consciousness, as you rise to Refined CC, the gap between the silent state of inner awareness and the active state of outer awareness decreases. Activity gets more and more infused with silence and unboundedness. This changes the perception as the unbounded nature of pure consciousness dominates the awareness.

My initial experience of Refined CC occurred a few years ago while walking in the forest in Iowa on a bright sunny day. A few minutes into my walk, I became aware that the whole environment was filled with soft golden light. I noticed that the trees, the shrubs, and other objects in the surroundings were particles of vibrating light energy. Everything was glowing, vibrating, and there was a feeling of expansion and deep silence, even though I could hear the birds chirping. I felt connected with everything. As I stood still and closed my eyes, an unbounded feeling of bliss, silence, and light-filled my awareness. When I opened my eyes, the inner feeling of silence, light, and unboundedness expanded to fill the surroundings. I realized that the light and unboundedness I experienced inside were the same as I was experiencing in the environment.

In chapters three and four, we saw that the finest level of the mind is the feeling and intuition level. As the conscious mind expands to include these finer levels of consciousness, the senses gain the ability to operate from these finer levels of creation, allowing you to see the finer structures of creation in the relative field of perception. This happens because the mind can now operate from the finest level of consciousness. You feel a deeper sense of connection with everything, which expands the heart and the feeling of love for all of creation and the Creator. For some, this concept may be challenging to grasp. To know it is to experience it. It is like trying to explain the taste of a fruit to someone who has never tasted the fruit before. This explanation can only go so far.

Refined Cosmic Consciousness continues to grow until you experience oneness with everything. We see everything in terms of myself. As you look at an object, you identify with the unified field that is at the basis of the object and realize that it is the same unified field within you. There is a constant awareness of expansion and silence that is present everywhere and in all things. This is the state of Unity Consciousness. The Vedic expression, I am That, all this is That, is now a living reality for the person in Unity Consciousness. This is the highest state of development and is a natural growth from Refined Cosmic Consciousness that occurs.

The values of achieving higher states of consciousness are many. First, the love and happiness you were seeking are now a constant in your daily life. Your creativity, energy, and perceptions are more refined. You are no longer needy and dependent on people's acceptance or appreciation of you. You can love freely without feeling attached. This gives you the freedom to live and love without expectation. You feel at home with everyone and everything. You no longer suffer from negative thoughts, feelings, and emotions but feel a closeness to God, the Creator, and a love for everyone. Bliss, freedom, creativity, and love dominate your life. According to Maharishi Mahesh Yogi, the founder of TM, this is your birthright.

Self-Realization and Religion

People often ask, Do you believe in God?. My answer is, yes, it's the only reality that there is. According to most religious teachings, God is love. God is the ultimate power, the Alpha and Omega, beginning and end of all things. It is said that God is here, there, and everywhere, and in all things. God is the creative intelligence, the life of everything in the universe.

In some of my talks to religious groups, I ask, Is God inside or outside of you?. Some in the audience would say within, others without. I would then ask, if you place a sieve in water, is the water inside the sieve, or is the sieve within the water? The answer is usually both. This is the same for God. Being here, there, and everywhere, God is within and without at the same time. For this to be true, the nature of God must be formless, beyond all change but responsible for all the changes and transformations we experience.

Throughout the centuries, men and women from all faiths who achieved enlightenment spoke of God as a living reality in their life. The beautiful expressions of St Theresa of Avila, St. Francis of Assisi, and St. Augustine mirror the feelings of the rishis and Maharishis of India. They all speak of discovering the light of God within and the deep connection they felt with God as a result.

The discovery of Quantum Physics shows that a field of infinite intelligence, energy, and creativity is at the source of everything in the universe. Interestingly, the spiritual teachers throughout the ages have all spoken about a similar field within. Could this be the discovery of God?

We have seen that the rise to higher states of consciousness opens the awareness to a greater appreciation of God's creation of others and increases our love, understanding, and compassion. Self-realization, therefore, fulfills the goal of all religions to grow in love, peace, happiness, and goodwill to all. I explore this subject in more detail in my book, Awaken To Your Divinity (Tin, Awaken To Your Divinity, 2015).

I often hear people say I want to become enlightened. The truth is you are already enlightened, but you have forgotten that you are. That is why enlightenment is called self-realization. You realize who you are and have always been. Self-realization is like a person slowly recovering from amnesia. Little by little, he remembers who he is, his family, friends, name, etc. Similarly, as we become more conscious of our nature as light beings, we begin to remember the bliss, peace, happiness, and freedom that we are. The unconditional love of God for everyone and everything grows in our awareness, and we are motivated by love to act.

Throughout this book, I have given examples of people from all walks of life who live in higher states of consciousness (Management, 2012). A growing number of scientific evidence shows the reality and practicality of rising to higher states of consciousness. Who would not want to have all this? However, to achieve it, you have to want it and work for it constantly. Otherwise, it will only be a fantasy.

CHAPTER 12

I Remember

My search for the answer to the question, who am I? led me on an interesting journey of self-discovery. As with any journey, there have been trials, disappointments, and victories along the way. All the techniques described in this book, I have practiced and still do many of them. I was fortunate to recognize the value of spiritual growth early in my adult life and study under Maharishi Mahesh Yogi, the founder of TM, for over twenty-five years. Maharishi explained the knowledge of higher states of consciousness and displayed it in his daily life.

As I gained more inner awareness, I remembered my true nature. The growing experience of inner peace, bliss, and love removed the need to chase after these daily lives. It s easier to accept people for who they are and to understand and sympathize with their struggles in life. There is an understanding that everyone is growing, evolving at their own pace. We are all souls on our own journey back home, and we all have our own karma to work out. Remembering your true nature as a Light-Being will go a long way in making your journey enjoyable and fruitful.

My experience of teaching thousands of people from all walks of life to meditate allowed me to see firsthand the transformation TM (www.TM.org, n.d.) created in their life. Many of my friends who are serious about their spiritual growth have experienced rising higher states of consciousness and continue to grow and enjoy more and more of life.

We all have our challenges and will continue to do so no matter the stage of our evolution. But as we grow, they will be seen as challenges rather than problems. We will tackle them with enthusiasm, knowing that they are there to assist us in growing and expressing our creative energies, rather than something that has come our way to hinder us. We see life as happening for us rather than to us.

Stress on our mind and body is like clouds that block out the sun, preventing us from appreciating the beauty of our inner, divine self. As we purify our physiology and psychology, we start to remember the glories of our kingdom of Heaven within, as there is no place, or a person, or anything as loving, beautiful, and nourishing as your inner self. That is why throughout the ages, it is said to know thy self.

For some, the path to self-realization may appear to be difficult and long, requiring some effort. I advise you not to give up or give in. It is well worth all the effort. I know from my experience and that of others who have undertaken the journey.

To achieve the goal, you have to nourish all aspects of life: the body, mind, intellect, feeling and emotions, and the self. Throughout the book, I have given techniques and suggested ways you can do this.

Knowledge is power. For knowledge to be useful we must act on the knowledge gained. Read and educate yourself about self-realization. Gain more direct experience of yourself through meditation. Nourish your body and mind with proper foods and exercises. And most important, take a deep look at your beliefs and values, as these create your perception of yourself and the world. Knowing how to master your emotions is important for spiritual growth.

Growing to higher states of consciousness requires a shift in the way we view ourselves and the world. We have to move away from the strictly Newtonian view of the world and embrace the more quantum mechanical view, where matter is energy and forces interacting. With the use of modern technologies such as cell phones, the internet, computers, and wireless, we are already unknowingly living in a quantum mechanical world. The various force fields created from the use of these technologies affect our minds and body.

A self-realized or enlightened individual acts, eats and indulges in activities like any other person. Outwardly, there may hardly be any sign that he/she is self-realized. We have become accustomed to thinking of enlightened individuals acting and dressing in a particular way. When a truly enlightened individual is looking and acting normally " dancing, singing, speaking loudly, or indulging in other mundane activity- we tend to dismiss him/her. One does not have to dress or act in a particular way that announces one's enlightened status. In fact, humility grows with enlightenment. There is no need to proclaim your status to anyone or the world. The self-realized individual enjoys the relative world like any other. The difference is he/she is not attached to the joys or sorrows of the world and is indifferent to the praises or abuses thrown their way. Their inner bliss and connection to the Divine is their constant source of nourishment.

So, my friends, meditate, breathe, eat healthily, exercise regularly, keep the company of those who share your values, and share the love. You are born to enjoy. Your life can be blissful.

Don t be an armchair philosopher. Take action every day to know yourself. Use your time wisely and aspire to make this world a better place in some way for everyone. May your life be a blessing to all.

REFERENCES

Brennan, b. A. (1988). Hands of light. Nrw York: Bantam Books.

Bruyere, R. L. (1994). Wheels of Light. New York: Fireside Book.

Christina L Ross, P. B. (2019). Energy Medicine: Current Status and Future Perspectives. Glob Adv Health Med. 2019; 8: 2164956119831221.

De La Warr, G. (1966). Matter in the Making. London, UK: Vincent Stuart Ltd.

Emoto, D. M. (2004). The Hidden Messages in Water. Atria Books.

Forem, J. (2012). Transcendental Meditation: The essential teachings of Maharishi Mahesh Yogi. New York: Hay House.

Frawley, D. D. (2003). Ayurveda and marma therapy. Wisconsin, USA: Lotus Press.

Frutjof, C. (1975). The Physics of Tao. Berkeley, CA, USA: Shambhala.

Hett, D. (29 May 2020). The Metacognitive Model of Posttraumatic Stress Disorder. https://www.psychreg.org/metacognitive-model-ptsd/.

Management, M. U. (2012). Invincible America Assembly Vol 1. Fairfield, Iowa: Maharishi University of Management Press.

Nader, D. T. (2000, 2014). Human Physiology Expression of Veda and Vedic Literature. Fairfield, Iowa, USA: Maharishi University of Management Press.

Schrott, D. E. (2016). Marma Therapy. London, UK: Jessica Kingsley Publishers.

Tansely, D. (1972). Radionics and the Subtle Anatomy of Man. Devon, England: Health Science Press,.

Tin, D. L. (2015). Awaken To Your Divinity. New Hampshire, USA: Mindstir Media.

Tin, D. L. (2015). Awaken To Your Divinity. New Hampshire USA: Mindstir Media.

University of Sussex, U. (March, 2017). Mind- wandering and alterations to default mode network connectivity when listening to naturalistic versus artificial sounds. Science Daily.

Wallace, R. B. (1971). A wakeful hypometabolic physiological state. American Journal of Physiology, 221(3): 795-799.

White, J. a. (1977). S., Future Science. New York, USA: Anchor Books,.

Yogi, M. M. (1963-2001). Science of Being and Art of Living. New York: Penguin Books, NY.

Yogi, M. M. (1971). Symposium on The Science of Creative Intelligence. Amherst, Massachusetts, U.S.A: http://www.excellenceinaction. globalgoodnews. com/2009/09-aug/aug15.html.

Zukav, G. (1979). The Dancing Wu Li Masters. New York, USA: William Morrow & Co.

ABOUT THE AUTHOR

Dr. David Lee Sheng Tin is passionate about assisting people in developing their full mental, emotional, physical, and spiritual potential. David is the author of *"Awaken to Your Divinity: Creating Your Emotional Fitness: The Missing Link to Spiritual Growth"* and *"Master Your Emotions-Transform Your Life,"* He is a board-Certified Holistic Health and Strategic Intervention Coach as well as a relationship and marriage educator.

Dr. Lee Sheng Tin is also a certified teacher of Transcendental Meditation and has studied Ayurveda and Traditional Chinese Medicine. He has been lecturing on the topic of human development, stress management, and healthy lifestyle to individuals, groups, and companies in the Caribbean and the USA for the past 25 years. Through his *"Blissfully Fit"* and *"Master Your Emotions Transform Your Life "* courses and personal coaching, he has been able to transform the lives of thousands of individuals by giving them the tools to make meaningful changes in their physical, emotional, and spiritual well-being.

Email: leeshengtind@gmail.com

www.ingramcontent.com/pod-product-compliance
Lightning Source LLC
Chambersburg PA
CBHW021645120626
46545CB00002B/720